NEAPTIDE

Taking Demeter and Persephone as its starting point, this new play, by the author of the controversial *Masterpieces*, mines the rich veins of mythology to tell the story of a woman's struggle to reconcile integrity, compromise and love in the face of prejudice and injustice.

Winner of the George Devine Award, *Neaptide* was premiered at the National Theatre in summer 1986.

'Miss Daniels has established herself as a distinct voice with real theatrical flair.'
Michael Coveney, *Financial Times*

by the same author
MASTERPIECES
RIPEN OUR DARKNESS & THE DEVIL'S GATEWAY

NEAPTIDE

SARAH DANIELS

A Methuen Paperback

Acknowledgement

My grateful thanks to Dr Phyllis Chesler for permission to quote from her interpretation of the Demeter myth and her book *Women and Madness* (Avon Books, 1972).

S.D.

First published in Great Britain as a paperback original in the Methuen New Theatrescript series in 1986 by Methuen London Ltd, 11 New Fetter Lane, London EC4P 4EE and in the United States of America by Methuen Inc, 29 West 35th Street, New York, NY 10001

Daniels, Sarah
    Neaptide.———(Methuen new theatrescript series)
    I. Title
    822'.914   PR6054.A52
    ISBN 0-413-57800-3

This play is dedicated to all the friends, both mothers and teachers who have shared their experiences with me, and whose help and encouragement have been invaluable.

Neaptide was first performed at the Cottesloe, National Theatre, London, on 26 June 1986, with the following cast:

CLAIRE, *27*	Jessica Turner
POPPY, *7, her daughter*	Lucy Speed
VAL, *29, Claire's sister*	Catherine Nielson
JOYCE, *57, mother of Claire and Val*	Mary Macleod
JEAN, *30, Claire's flatmate*	Sheila Kelly
SID, *58, father of Claire and Val*	Anthony Douse
LAWRENCE, *31, Claire's ex-husband*	Michael Bray
COLIN, *30, Val's husband*	Peter Attard
WALTER } *4, Val's twin sons*	Marc Bellamy
SID JUNIOR	Richard Lawrence
JUSTIN, *5* } *Jean's sons*	John Sinclair
SPENCER, *6*	Ruben Patino
BEATRICE GRIMBLE, *51, headmistress*	Janet Whiteside
LINDA FELLOWS, *33, games mistress*	Theresa Watson
ANNETTE POLLARD, *54, domestic science teacher*	Jean Watts
MARION LANDSDOWNE, *32, needlework teacher*	Anna Keaveney
CYRIL BARRETT, *64, physics teacher*	Anthony Douse
ROGER CUNNINGHAM, *29, English teacher*	Roderick Smith
DIANE } *17, sixth form pupils*	Miranda Foster
TERRI	Jacquetta May

YOUNG DOCTOR, *male*   Peter Attard
OLDER DOCTOR, *male*   Anthony Douse
NURSE, *female*   }   Jacquetta May
CLERK OF THE COURT, *female*   Miranda Foster
BARRISTER, *male*   Peter Attard
FLORRIE, *voice only*   Jean Watts

Directed by John Burgess
Designed by Alison Chitty

The play is set in an outer London suburb. The events take place in March 1983.

PART ONE

Scene One

A hospital. TWO DOCTORS, *both men,
one some years older than the other, stand by
VAL's bed. A female* NURSE *hovers in the
background. They are all oblivious to VAL's
first speech.*

VAL: The performers in this pit are as old as
the witchcraft trials. Centre stage. The
powerful male Doctor-Inquisitor. In the
wings, a subservient female
Handmaiden-Nurse. Stranded on a mud
flat, myself, a Witch-Patient.

The DOCTORS *appear to be in the midst
of a deep conversation when* JOYCE
enters.

OLDER DOCTOR (*with genuine
concern*): I'm afraid you can't see your
daughter at the moment, she needs plenty
of rest. Perhaps you would care to wait
outside? (*With a gesture he indicates to the*
NURSE *to show* JOYCE *out of the room.
Exit* JOYCE *with* NURSE. *Then to the*
YOUNGER DOCTOR:) I wasn't on
duty last night. Strictly speaking, March
will see to this one.

YOUNGER DOCTOR (*smiles*): Hare
March?

OLDER DOCTOR: Don't tell me, on top
of everything else our quack colleague is
German.

YOUNGER DOCTOR: I meant as in 'Mad
as . . .'

OLDER DOCTOR: Oh, I'm with you now.
Hum yes. (*Shaking his head over* VAL.)
Probably have her flung out inside a
week.

YOUNGER DOCTOR: With disarming
success, no doubt.

OLDER DOCTOR: And who'll have to
mop up the long-term backlash. Hum?
Caught in the unfortunate irony of
psychiatric policy – concentration of
short-term solutions. Our analyst friend is
careful not to contravene that.

YOUNGER DOCTOR (*drily*): What's the
difference between a cow chewing the
cud and a therapist chewing gum? The
cow has an intelligent look on its face.

OLDER DOCTOR (*wryly*): I'll leave it to
you then. (*He exits.*)

YOUNGER DOCTOR (*calls off*): Staff.

The NURSE *enters.*

NURSE: Yes, doctor.

YOUNGER DOCTOR: Did you manage
to dredge the social worker's report up?

NURSE (*offers him the medical notes which
include a photocopy of the social worker's
report*): Yes, I'm afraid there's not much
to go on though.

YOUNGER DOCTOR (*taking the file*): Is
there ever? (*He sighs. Flicking through
them.*) Huh, that's a fat lot of good. (*He
hands the notes back to her.*) Still, make it
available to Dr March, we mustn't allow
accusations of unco-operation to fly
around the ward. Children?

NURSE: Doctor?

YOUNGER DOCTOR: Has she got any
offspring?

NURSE: Yes, two.

YOUNGER DOCTOR: And do we know,
pray, who is looking after them?

NURSE: The maternal grandmother is to
collect them from the nursery and look
after them until the father gets in from
work. In fact she's outside now.

YOUNGER DOCTOR: Who? Who is?

NURSE: Mrs Jones's mother. Shall I tell
her she can come in.?

YOUNGER DOCTOR: Oh yes, yes.

They both exit.

NURSE (*as she goes through the door*): You
can come in now, Mrs Roberts.

Enter JOYCE. *She crosses to the bed,
pulls up a chair and sits down very
unconfidently.*

JOYCE: Hello love, how are you feeling?
(*Pause.*) Don't worry about the boys,
they're fine. We took them to playschool
this morning. They were ever so good, no
tears or nothing and I'll collect them for as
long – (*She stops herself.*) – for as long as
they want to go. (*Pause.*) Colin's
rearranging his timetable at work so not
to worry. He sends all his love. (*Pause.*)
He's beside himself, I mean he's very
concerned. Well, we all are, we all are.

For you. That you get well, back to your old self. (*Finally*:) Have you got a message for him? (*Silence.*) Val?

VAL (*quietly*): Here I sit, mad as a hatter with nothing to do but either become madder and madder or else recover enough of my sanity to be allowed back to the world that drove me mad.

JOYCE (*shocked*): I don't think I can remember all that. What on earth possessed you to come out with a mouthful like that?

VAL: I didn't say it.

JOYCE (*gently, slightly patronisingly*): Oh, Val, who did then? The washstand?

VAL: Some woman years ago. I don't think there are any original states of mind left to reclaim.

JOYCE (*sighs*): Val, love, this won't do. Now, I've brought you a clean nightie and two flannels.

Scene Two

Afternoon. Sunday. Two days previously. CLAIRE's living-room. CLAIRE is sitting in an armchair. POPPY is sitting on her lap. She has been reading Mrs Plug the Plumber to CLAIRE. There is a Mother's Day card, which POPPY has made, on the mantlepiece.

POPPY (*reading*): Ah well, all in a day's work, said Mrs Plug. I'm going to go home and have a slap-up supper, this job is driving me round the bend. (*She slaps the book shut.*)

CLAIRE (*laughs*): Poppy, it does not end like that.

POPPY: I know. I thought it was boring for you.

CLAIRE: Now, have you got your nan's present ready?

POPPY: Yes, I've hid it behind the chair.

CLAIRE: Good.

POPPY: It's your turn.

CLAIRE: What is?

POPPY: It's your turn to read me a story, you promised.

CLAIRE: It's just that they'll be here soon.

POPPY: You promised.

CLAIRE: Okay, okay, which one . . .

POPPY: Pepsi-phone.

CLAIRE: Persephone.

CLAIRE *picks up a book.*

In the beginning, if there ever was such a time, Demeter, the goddess of life, gave birth to four daughters, whom she named Persephone, Psyche, Athena and Artemis. The world's first children were unremarkably happy. To amuse their mother – with whom they were all passionately in love – they invented language, music, laughter – and many more useful and boisterous activities.
   One morning Persephone menstruated. That afternoon, Demeter's daughters gathered flowers to celebrate the loveliness of the event. A chariot thundered, then clattered into their midst. It was Hades, the middle-aged god of death, come to take Persephone, come to carry her off to be his queen, to sit beside him in the realm of non-being below the earth, come to commit the first act of violence earth's children had ever known.

Pause.

. . . and thus they each discovered that in shame and sorrow childhood ends, and that nothing remains the same.
   Persephone's sisters came home without her. Demeter raged and wept. She bound up her hair and turned wanderer, but could not find her eldest daughter anywhere on earth.

POPPY: No, because she wasn't on the world, she was underneath it.

CLAIRE: Finally the sun spoke and told Demeter what had happened, that her daughter was married and a queen. He counselled her:
   'Why mourn the natural fate of daughters – to leave their mother's home, to lose their virginity, marry, and to give birth to children?'

POPPY: Silly sun.

CLAIRE: Demeter was grieved beyond and before reasoning.

POPPY: She was vivid.

CLAIRE: What?

POPPY: Raging mad.

CLAIRE: Oh, livid.

POPPY: Yes, hopping livid.

CLAIRE: Remembering an oracle's prophecy of a splitting, a scattering and an exile, she said to the sun:
'Yea, if that be the natural fate of daughters, let all mankind perish. Let there be no crops, no grain, no corn, if this maiden is not returned to me.'
And she stopped the world.

POPPY: Brillo, that's my favourite bit.

CLAIRE: And because Demeter was a powerful goddess, her wishes were commands and Persephone returned, but she still had to visit her husband once a year and during that time no crops would grow. However, neither husband nor child nor stranger would ever claim her as his own. Persephone belonged to her mother. That was Demeter's gift to herself.

Silence.

POPPY: Did she really stop the world?

CLAIRE: Why do you think nothing can grow in winter and all the leaves fall off the trees?

POPPY: Do you really believe that? Really and truly?

CLAIRE: Well, I certainly like it better than *Cinderella* or *Sleeping Beauty.*

POPPY: Don't stop there, what happened to all the others?

JOYCE (*off*): Hello? Anyone at home?

CLAIRE: In here, Mum. (*To* POPPY:) When they've gone it's bath and bed, okay?

POPPY: Aw mum.

Enter JOYCE *and* VAL.

JOYCE: You should really keep the door locked. I could've been anyone. Hello love. (*She kisses* CLAIRE.) Hello Poppy.

POPPY *hugs* JOYCE, *then goes and gets* JOYCE's *present which is a daffodil in a brightly painted pot.*

CLAIRE: I'm glad you could make it, Val.

VAL *smiles. They sit down.*

JOYCE: We let your father and Colin go for a drink, so it's just us together. (*To* CLAIRE:) Thought you'd appreciate that. Now don't go putting the kettle on. We've had so many cups of tea it's a wonder I've not turned into a watering can.

POPPY (*presenting* JOYCE *with her present*): Happy Mother's Day, Nan.

JOYCE (*very pleased*): Oh Poppy, thank you. It's lovely. Did you grow it yourself?

POPPY (*considering this*): Well, I put it in a cupboard under the stairs for ages but it grew by itself really. I painted the pot though.

JOYCE: And very nicely too. Who are these?

POPPY (*pointing at the pictures*): This one is you, Nan. This one is Val and this is Sybil and –

JOYCE (*correcting*): Aunty Val and Aunty Sybil.

CLAIRE: Yes and this one is Claire.

JOYCE (*correcting*): Mummy.

POPPY (*affirming*): Yes, that's right, my Mum.

JOYCE: Honestly, Claire, if children grow up using their parents' names it's no wonder they end up rioting.

CLAIRE (*handing* JOYCE *a wrapped gift*): Happy Mother's Day.

JOYCE: Oh thank you. (*Pleasantly:*) Gawd, I'm a bit frightened to open it. I'm never sure what I'll get from you. What with tea towels about sinking into his sink.

CLAIRE: That was years ago.

JOYCE: It was still too late then. I've spent the best part of my life with my arms in Fairy Liquid. Anyway, I just hope it's something I can show your father.

CLAIRE: If you usually show him the cardigans people give you from Marks and Spencer before you change them for thermal underwear, yes, you can.

JOYCE: All right, don't take . . .

POPPY: Oh, open it, Nan, open it.

JOYCE (*opening it and finding it is a cardigan from Marks and Spencer*): Oh it's very nice, thank you, Claire. And I got a card from Sybil yesterday.

VAL: Oh Sybil, Sybil, Sybil. What a name to call a child, don't dribble Sybil.

JOYCE: There's no need to be like that, Val. She was named after my mother and you know full well I didn't want any of you named after her. God knows your christening was a trauma and a half, Val, but when it came to Sybil's I just didn't have the strength to take another scene behind the font. Anyway, I don't know if they have such a thing as Mother's Day out there, but my card had the Statue of Liberty on it, so I don't know whether that was by design or coincidence, but it only says she'll ring tonight. I only hope she gets the time lapse right. I have no desire to be wished 'Happy Mother's Day' at three o'clock tomorrow morning, thank you very much.

CLAIRE: I'm sure she won't. Do give her my love.

JOYCE: Yes, of course. You know it's on an island, don't you? Did you know that?

CLAIRE: Manhattan?

JOYCE: I know that's an island don't I? No, the Statue of Liberty is stuck out in the water on something no bigger than your garden and, you know, here was I thinking it was like Eros slap bang in the middle of things. I said to Sid, I did, just as well I've never been on Mastermind not knowing something like that. He laughed, that's why I married him, he's a good laugh, your father.

CLAIRE: You should see the Statue of Liberty for yourself, Sybil's always saying she'd like you to go over and visit.

JOYCE: What with? That's what I'd like to know.

CLAIRE: You can get quite a cheap fare and there's Dad's redundancy money.

JOYCE: We can't go throwing that about traipsing round the world. Have you lost your senses? And what's your father s'posed to do – go down the dole and say, 'Be good lads and just pop the next few Giros in the post to New York'? That would make them roll in the aisles, I'm sure.

CLAIRE: Sorry, it was only . . .

JOYCE: An idea. Yes, well, the very idea I'm not so sure as I want to go over there in the first place and I can't for the life of me fathom why Sybil flounced off there. I still wake up of a night in a cold sweat praying she's not been mugged.

CLAIRE: Oh, Mum.

JOYCE: I do, you know, I do, and fancy, ask you, of all the places to live in New York she ends up in somewhere called SoHo. Other people over there at least have those normal numbered addresses like 42nd Street.

CLAIRE: She's a journalist, nothing else.

JOYCE: I know it's only a name and what in a name but you don't have to face the neighbours: 'And where's your daughter living these days, Mrs Roberts?' 'Well, actually, in New York's SoHo.' Well, the way they look you'd think I'd just said she'd dropped dead.

CLAIRE: So how are you?

JOYCE: And where's that err . . . Joan?

CLAIRE: Jean. She went to her mother's for the weekend.

JOYCE: Did she take the boys with her?

CLAIRE: No, actually they're staying with Riq until tonight.

JOYCE: Oh, is he still hanging around?

CLAIRE: She and Riq have been lovers for five years.

JOYCE: It's about time they jolly well got married then.

CLAIRE: That's their business, Mum.

JOYCE: And, it's a good deal better than some other people's arrangements.

CLAIRE (gently): Now, Mum.

JOYCE (sighs): Still it's your life, each to their own, live and let live, that's what I always say.

VAL (deliberate sarcasm): Ha. Ha.

CLAIRE: Val?

VAL (snaps): Fine, fine, I'm fine.

JOYCE: Course you are, course she is, just not been herself, right now . . . lately (To CLAIRE:) Now don't you start probing and upsetting everyone. I notice nobody bothers to ask how I am. I suppose I'm not worth bothering with.

CLAIRE (*curtly*): I just did, only you ignored it.

JOYCE: Sometimes, frankly, it's just as well not to ask. Life's not a bowl of anything much. Especially with neighbours banging away into the night – they've even got an hydraulic cat-flap, God alone knows why, on the twelfth floor. Still, moaning about it doesn't get you anywhere. Laugh and the world laughs with you, weep and you weep alone, that's my motto.

VAL (*quietly*): One by one we all file on down the narrow aisles of pain alone.

JOYCE: Pardon? Val?

VAL: Thought I'd finish where you started.

JOYCE (*choosing not to take this up*): What a life, I ask you. I tell you I need one of those *Help* programmes all to myself. I thank God I'm not a Catholic, that's all I can say, not that he's not the best pope so far, this one.

VAL (*flatly*): Hurray, hurray, it's Mother's Day.

JOYCE: What's got into you these days, Val? You used to be so sensitive.

CLAIRE: Mum!

JOYCE (*to* CLAIRE): Which is more than I can say for you, I'm afraid, young lady.

CLAIRE: Woman.

JOYCE: Oh Claire, where is all this nit-picking getting you? (*Firmly:*) I'll tell you one thing for nothing: when you were born, they didn't say to me, 'Mrs Roberts, you've got a lovely little baby woman.'

CLAIRE: I'm sure they didn't say 'You've got a lovely little baby lady' either.

JOYCE: Whereas Val could have been a poet, couldn't you, dear? I'll never forget when I met one of her lecturers, he said you've got a potential . . .

VAL (*flatly*): The distortion of abortion is a Catholic contortion from which I can only conceive that the Papist is a rapist.

JOYCE: Well, you haven't been feeling very well lately, have you? No, no, we won't go into that now. Everyday in every way getting better all the time. You look much better than when I last saw you. Doesn't she?

CLAIRE: Did you ever enrol for those cookery classes, Mum?

JOYCE: What went wrong? Oh, what went wrong? I didn't mind that you were all girls, oh no I didn't. I just wished that you'd all turn out like those Brontë sisters. (*VAL and* CLAIRE *exchange exasperated looks.*) Yes, well, that was a load of pie-in-the-sky nonsense. For a start their father was a priest. I don't suppose for one minute that many great lady – (*She looks at* CLAIRE.) – women novelists had dockers, unemployed, ones at that, for fathers. (*To* CLAIRE:) There, that's what you should be going on about in your sociological stuff.

CLAIRE (*controlled*): That's what I do go on about, Mum, only my analysis isn't quite so succinct.

JOYCE: And that's another thing, I bet Charlotte Brontë didn't talk to her mother like that.

CLAIRE: If I remember rightly her mother died when she was seven.

JOYCE: And that's where I'll be, in the grave, thanks to you. Things you've put me through.

CLAIRE (*through clenched teeth*): Mother, please.

JOYCE: It wasn't for the want of trying, my girl, didn't I always encourage you to play with the vicar's daughter?

VAL *laughs out loud,* CLAIRE *suppresses a smile.*

Now what are you laughing at? They were a very nice family. Mark and Harriet – wonderful people, and I hoped by you mixing with their daughter Mary some of the respectability might rub off.

CLAIRE: Mum? Mary had three abortions by the time she was eighteen.

JOYCE: Well, with a name like that she was hardly blessed. Still, it's quite something to have your father called by God like he was.

VAL: Probably what he heard was a dog with a hairlip calling 'Mark, Mark'.

JOYCE: Val! Please not in front of the child.

POPPY: Did you know, Nan, 'god' spells dog backwards.

JOYCE: Poppy!

CLAIRE: Poppy, I think you've overstepped the mark.

POPPY: But it's true.

JOYCE: Is this what it comes down to, one of my daughters calls the Pope a sod, the other says he's a rapist, and my granddaughter goes one further and calls God a dog. Heaven help us, on Mothering Sunday as well.

Silence.

POPPY: I didn't call God a dog.

CLAIRE: Mum, we've done all right. Everything considered. And we owe that to you. (*To* POPPY.) No, I know you didn't, love.

JOYCE (*to* CLAIRE): I've taken enough blame for everything. Don't start on me.

CLAIRE: Look Val and I went to university, neither you nor Dad went there. And we weren't pushed into it like loads of others. Mum, you were always saying don't get married like you did at nineteen and regret it.

JOYCE: Regret it? Regret it? What have I got to regret? I might have said don't get married at *sixteen*, but I didn't say don't get married at all or fornicate or emigrate or crack up or go the other way or whatever. My God, I wanted three daughters like the Brontës and I ended up with a family fit for a Channel Four documentary. Regrets, me? It's you lot that should have regrets.

CLAIRE: I give up.

JOYCE: Now you know how I feel – I gave up a long time ago.

CLAIRE: Why do you have to criticise me all the time?

JOYCE: Me? Criticise? Just what do I criticise you about?

Enter JEAN *behind* JOYCE.

CLAIRE: Hi, Jean.

JOYCE: Personal cleanliness is the last thing I'd criticise you for – you can tell that by your fingernails – spotless. (*She sees* JEAN.) Oh, hello Joan – did you have a nice time?

JEAN (*flatly*): I went to my mother's.

JOYCE: Not a good recipe for success, if my mother was alive today she'd wish herself dead again. Poor woman, God rest her soul.

JEAN *sees the way the conversation is going and exits.*

Not that there's not plenty I could be having a go at you for.

CLAIRE: Perhaps not now, eh, Mum?

JOYCE: I wonder whether my feelings ever get taken into consideration.

CLAIRE: Mum!

JOYCE: Don't worry, I know – L–I–T–T–L–E E–A–R–S.

Pause.

POPPY: Little ears, what does that mean?

JOYCE: Nothing, love, it's slang for Nanny's got a big mouth.

POPPY: Mum? There's only three, Demeter had four.

CLAIRE: You're the fourth.

POPPY (*pointing at* JOYCE): So you're Demeter.

JOYCE: Don't point dear, it's rude.

POPPY (*nodding towards* VAL): You're Psyche and Aunty Sybil can be Athena.

VAL: Do you learn this at school?

POPPY: No, Claire – (*She looks at* JOYCE.) – Mummy tells me.

JOYCE: Course, Val did her degree in the classics, didn't you love.

VAL: I never finished it.

JOYCE: No, but only because nature had something better designed for you, didn't it? Not that your father and I weren't upset at the time because we were, we were, but Colin is a very decent man and he's done the best thing by you, he has. You have a marvellous husband and a lovely family, sometimes I think you don't realise how lucky you are, I don't.

CLAIRE: Did you ever enrol for those brass rubbing classes, Mum?

JOYCE: Oh, that's just typical of you, stick

your head in the sand, hear no evil, see no evil, but (*She stops herself.*) I tell you this much: a social worker had never so much as put a finger on the doorbell until . . .

CLAIRE (*harshly*): Mum, leave it out, please.

JOYCE: It's all very well you saying, 'Mum, please', but that won't solve anything.

CLAIRE: And nor will your carrying on about it.

JOYCE: Honestly. Have you no shame?

CLAIRE (*slowly*): Will you stop picking on me.

JOYCE: Me? Me? Picking on you? Huh, I like that. It's usually only drunk and insane mothers who are considered unfit for parental control.

CLAIRE: Shut up.

VAL: Stop it. Stop it. Stop it.

JOYCE: There, look now, what you've done now. Look.

CLAIRE: I haven't upset anyone. If anyone's upset anyone . . .

JOYCE: What about me and my ties with her?

CLAIRE (*shouts*): Drop it please.

Enter SID.

SID: Drop what? I came straight in, the door was open.

JOYCE (*startled*): Oh Sidney, love, it's you. Where's Colin.

SID: Trying to park the car. This must be getting into a trendy area, can always tell when the Citroëns are double-parked. Hello there, Val, Claire. And how's Poppy?

POPPY: Hello Grandad – you can be – (*To* CLAIRE:) Who can he be? I know, Zeus.

SID: That's my cleverest granddaughter. (*To* CLAIRE:) And if I'm Zeus, who are you?

POPPY: Pepsi-phone.

SID: Now me, I'm somewhat Carling-Black-Label-prone myself.

POPPY: Where have you been?

SID: Tell who this one's taking after. (*He looks at* JOYCE.)

JOYCE: He's been to the pub, as if we need ask, when he knows full well that we haven't got the money for him to go swilling beer down his neck with.

SID: You know what her latest economy is now? Eh? Keeps the curtains drawn so the sunlight doesn't fade the carpet.

JOYCE: Someone's got to budget.

SID: Nothing will budge it either, the pattern will be stuck on it a long time after we're gone. Hey, Poppy, do you want to sit on my knee?

POPPY: No thank you.

SID (*to* CLAIRE): If that kid grows up with any weird ideas, I'l kill you.

CLAIRE: Oh really? Not before I kill you, I suppose.

JOYCE: What are you going to do, stab him to death with your 'Women Against Violence' badge?

VAL (*to* SID): Leave her alone.

SID (*to* CLAIRE): D'you hear me?

CLAIRE: Father, your theories of biologically-inherited traits are as about as informed as your vocabulary.

SID: Don't sauce me, girl, you're not too big to feel the back of my hand.

CLAIRE: You what?

Enter COLIN.

JOYCE: Ah ha, hello Colin, how lovely to see you. We were just going to make a nice cup of tea – would you like one?

COLIN: No thanks, if it's all the same. It's just that I've left the boys with the neighbours. How are you feeling, Val?

VAL: Fine.

COLIN: Oh well, no worse, that's better. Are you ready?

SID: I don't know what I meant to say – you didn't show up for that game of arrows last Tuesday?

COLIN: Sorry about that, but I like to spend time with my family.

JOYCE (*to the* WOMEN): What a lovely man. (*To* SID:) He's got better things to do with his money than booze it away, not like some I could mention.

SID: You want to know something, my wife's so mean, when she tried to get the last bit out of the toothpaste tube she broke her foot.

COLIN *feels he has to smile.*

JOYCE: What are you coming as, Les Dawson?

SID: Wish I was.

JOYCE: You know very well that's not true. I cut them in half and use a rolling pin. (*To the* WOMEN:) He loves me really.

SID: I'll tell you another thing.

VAL: Shut up.

COLIN: I think we'd better be making tracks. The boys will probably be demolishing next-door's patio by now.

JOYCE (*to* VAL): Don't worry about your father, he's just trying to do his impression of a river – small at the head and big at the mouth.

COLIN (*to* SID): Can I give you a lift?

SID: Very kind of you, boy. (*To* JOYCE:) Come on then, let's be having yer.

CLAIRE: Bye, Dad.

POPPY: Bye, Grandad.

SID: See you soon, Poppy, Claire.

COLIN: Shall we make a move?

CLAIRE: Take care, Val.

VAL *nods. Exit* VAL, COLIN *and* SID.

JOYCE: We must have a family get-together more often. It's been lovely to see you. Thanks very much for my presents.

POPPY: S'okay. Bye, Nan.

JOYCE *kisses* POPPY *and then* CLAIRE.

CLAIRE: Bye, Mum. And stop worrying.

JOYCE: What else am I supposed to do? What else can I do? Sometimes you forget.

SID (*overlapping, off*): Come on, stop jawing, girl.

JOYCE: Any rate, enough said. Bye. (*Exit* JOYCE.)

POPPY *and* CLAIRE *sit down.*

CLAIRE: Phew.

POPPY: I don't know which one is more crackers, Nan or Aunty Val.

CLAIRE: Val's not crackers, love. She's depressed.

POPPY: What's that?

CLAIRE: It's . . . it's . . . I think it's like when you feel angry but can't show it, so you feel sort of sad.

Enter JEAN.

JEAN: Coast clear?

CLAIRE: Just about. Where's Riq?

JEAN: He's putting the boys to bed.

CLAIRE: Come on Poppy. I'll run the bath for you.

POPPY: I'll do it.

CLAIRE: Okay. I'll come up for a chat when you're in bed.

POPPY: I'll shout when I'm ready. (*Exit* POPPY.)

CLAIRE: Was your weekend really awful?

JEAN: Worse. How was yours?

CLAIRE: Very quiet, apart from this evening; Mum's beside herself.

Enter LAWRENCE.

JEAN: We should have locked the back door.

LAWRENCE: I want a word with my wife. Alone.

JEAN: Your wife doesn't live here.

LAWRENCE: Claire. Clever clogs.

CLAIRE: Lawrence, how many more times. This sort of confrontation is s'posed to be done through our solicitors.

LAWRENCE: I want a word with my ex-wife in private.

CLAIRE: Say what you want to say and go.

LAWRENCE: I want to see my daughter then.

CLAIRE: Don't be so irresponsible.

LAWRENCE: It was my turn to have her this weekend.

CLAIRE (*quietly angry*): No, Lawrence, it was your turn last weekend, but you rang up and cancelled it because your wife . . .

LAWRENCE (*overlapping*): She does have a name you know.

CLAIRE: Abigail had to go and look after her dad.

LAWRENCE: So I should have seen Poppy this weekend.

CLAIRE (*as if to a child*): No, Lawrence, last weekend and next weekend. (*Then:*) For Christ's sake, it's Mother's Day. Even in your perversity, do you not think it's somehow fitting for my daughter to be with me today?

LAWRENCE: You're going to have plenty of time to be sorry enough . . .

JEAN (*coldly*): I thought I told you to leave.

LAWRENCE (*to* CLAIRE): We've got everything sewn up.

CLAIRE: You think?

LAWRENCE: The sordid details are going to make you look unfit to have a goldfish bowl in your care.

CLAIRE: I should have taken an injunction out.

LAWRENCE: Not worth it now.

They both look at him.

Don't worry, I'm going.

Exit LAWRENCE.

JEAN: How many more times?

CLAIRE: At least it will be out of his hands soon. Whatever happens he won't be able to just drop in.

JEAN: I can't believe the way he carries on.

Pause.

CLAIRE (*changing the subject*): Do you think you and Riq will ever live together?

JEAN: You sound as bad as my mother.

CLAIRE: Sound as bad as mine come to that.

JEAN: I've got everything I want from a relationship. So has he, except he has to do his own washing.

CLAIRE: Let's get everything ready for tomorrow.

JEAN: Sunday evening, ugg, work

tomorrow, it's so depressing.

CLAIRE: My job's the one thing I've got going for me.

JEAN: And you're good at it. How's po-faced Marion these days?

CLAIRE: She found some obscene graffiti last week. Probably kept her going all weekend.

JEAN: Any excuse for her to go tittle-tattling to the Head. Funny how some people never grow out of attention-seeking.

CLAIRE (*mock dramatic*): And worse, she thought the culprit was one of the lower sixth in my group.

JEAN (*smiles*): Sounds nasty.

CLAIRE: It'll blow over.

JEAN (*getting up*): Come on, I'll set the table, anything to make breakfast more bearable.

Scene Three

The next morning. Breakfast bedlam. JUSTIN, SPENCER *and* POPPY *sit at the table.* CLAIRE *is trying to clear away as they go along.* JEAN *is trying to cut* JUSTIN'*s hair.* JUSTIN *and* SPENCER *are fighting over the cut-out model on the back of the Rice Krispies packet.*

SPENCER (*grabbing the packet; to* JUSTIN *so* JEAN *can't hear*): It's mine.

JUSTIN (*screams*): Arhh, he's not getting it, is he Mum? Mum, is he? It's mine. It's mine. I want it. Mum? Mum? Tell him.

JEAN (*twisting* JUSTIN'*s head back in position*): Hold still, Justin.

SPENCER: It's my turn, you promised me, Mum, not him, didn't you, you did, you did, in Sainsbury's.

JUSTIN: You liar. She never. It's my turn, put it back, it's mine.

SPENCER (*jeering*): Ha ha hee hee. I've got it now so it belongs to me nar nar.

JUSTIN: It's not, you can't have it. It's still full up. Put it back.

SPENCER: Finders keepers, losers weepers.

JUSTIN: Give it me. Now.

SPENCER: No.

JUSTIN *makes a lunge for the packet. The scissors miss his ear by a fraction. JEAN grabs the packet and puts it back on the table.*

JEAN: Just piss off. (*She puts the scissors down and sits to eat her own cereal.*)

JUSTIN (*to* SPENCER): She told you to piss off. Piss off. (*He puts his tongue out.*) She told you to piss off.

POPPY (*telling* CLAIRE): Jean said 'piss off'.

CLAIRE: Morning isn't the best time for any of us.

SPENCER *has picked up the scissors and is cutting out the back of the packet with little regard for the contents.*

JUSTIN: Mum! Mum! He's doing it, look, look, tell him off.

JEAN (*rounds on* SPENCER *and grabs the scissors*): Behave or I'll cut your head off.

JUSTIN: She's going to do a Henry the Eighth on you.

JEAN: Justin, shut up.

CLAIRE *and* JEAN *sit down to their respective bowls of cereal.* SPENCER *and* JUSTIN *continue to prod and pinch each other until* SPENCER *bangs his spoon into* JUSTIN*'s bowl of Rice Krispies.* JEAN, *in response, flicks a spoonful of her cereal into* SPENCER*'s face.*

JUSTIN (*laughs*): You got paid back.

SPENCER: What did you do that for, Mum? Mum? What did you do that for?

CLAIRE: Jean?

JEAN (*foul mood*): I haven't got three degrees and spent seven years training to be an educational psychologist not to know how to treat my kids.

SPENCER (*wingeing*): You said you would cut my head off.

JEAN: Spencer, talk properly.

SPENCER: And you said 'piss off'.

JEAN: If I hear one more word out of you, you'll be reading about how you drowned in a bowl of Rice Krispies in next week's *Beezer*.

JUSTIN: He couldn't read about it if he was dead.

JEAN: What have I told you about trying to be too clever, Justin? (JUSTIN *opens his mouth to reply.*) I don't care. Shut it. We're late as it is. (*To* CLAIRE:) I'll give you and Poppy a lift if you like.

CLAIRE: Thanks, we'll both get told off if we're not there before the bell.

POPPY: Oh, they don't mind. They know you're a teacher.

CLAIRE: Well, my headmistress knows I'm a mother, but it doesn't seem to work that way around.

JEAN (*to* CLAIRE): What about having time off?

CLAIRE: I've got it all worked out.

JEAN: That's good, well, you know.

CLAIRE: Not that Lawrence wouldn't rearrange the school timetable if he could to make it as awkward as possible all round. Bastard.

POPPY: My dad isn't a bastard. I'll tell him you said that.

CLAIRE: You can Poppy. Sadly, he's heard me call him worse things that that.

JUSTIN: What's a bastard?

CLAIRE: Sorry, Justin, I used the wrong word. I was angry but that word was inappropriate – wrong.

JUSTIN: Yes, but what's . . .

POPPY: When Jean's angry with Riq she calls him a wanker.

CLAIRE (*firmly*): Thank you, Poppy.

JUSTIN: What's a wanker? (*Pause.*) What's a wanker?

CLAIRE (*looks at* JEAN, *who has bowed out of the conversation in favour of charging over the mess on the floor with a carpet sweeper*): It's . . . er . . . someone who err . . . wastes a lot of time on themselves.

JUSTIN (*to* SPENCER): Wanker. Wanker.

SPENCER: Takes one to know one, you are, yourself, you are . . .

JEAN: Right out to the car both of you. (*Brandishing scissors.*) Or I'll make both your nostrils into one.

USTIN: Wank off. Wank off.

EAN: Just one big hole.

The BOYS *run to the door.*

PENCER: Wouldn't be as big as your mouth.

The BOYS *exit.*

EAN (*shouts after them*): And don't tempt me by playing under the wheels. Stand by the door. (*To* CLAIRE:) I'll just get my things together and I'll be with you. I don't know which goddess is responsible for Mondays, but I could strangle her.

LAIRE (*helps* POPPY *on with her coat*): Ready, love?

OPPY: She forgot the scissors.

LAIRE (*smiles*): I think she was only joking.

cene Four

taff room. Before school. MARION *and* NNETTE *are marking exercise books.* YRIL *is reading the sports pages in* The imes. LINDA *is sorting out arm bands.* OGER *appears to be trying to mate two aper clips, there is a knock at the door.*

YRIL (*without looking up*): Go away and come back after the nuclear war or Easter, whichever happens to be the latter.

NNETTE: Honestly, Cyril, it's lucky they can't hear you.

YRIL (*mumbles*): Blasted kids.

Another knock.

OGER: Well, whose turn is it?

LL OTHERS: Yours.

OGER: Okay, okay. (*He goes to the door and opens it to* DIANE *and* TERRI:) Yes, girls what can I do for you?

IANE: We'd like the key to the stationery cupboard in the commerce room.

OGER: What? (*He looks at his watch.*) Is this shift work? We haven't had assembly yet.

IANE: Miss Grimble wants some stuff run

off and we didn't finish it on Friday.

ROGER: And where's Miss Whatsit Evans who's supposed to be in charge of that room?

TERRI: She's off sick again.

ROGER: Well, I don't know . . .

TERRI: Ahh, go on, Sir.

ROGER: Don't go away. (*He goes to the board, which has various keys on it, and selects one.*)

ANNETTE (*curtly*): Really, I think you should go with them, Mr Cunningham. Keys are not to be taken from this room without being accompanied by the teacher.

ROGER (*defensively*): But Miss Do-da Evans is off sick.

ANNETTE: Precisely.

DIANE: We'll bring them straight back, Miss.

ROGER (*giving* DIANE *the key*): Here you are, but if we read that the Russian warheads were made from two dozen gross of Her Majesty's drawing pins, we'll know who the culprits were, ha ha!

TERRI (*forcing a laugh*): Thank you, Sir.

MARION (*calls*): Please shut the door.

No response.

CYRIL: They're all born in a barn.

ANNETTE: Someone should make sure the key is retrieved. Those two aren't renowned for their reliability. (*She sighs.*) I don't see why it should always be me. (*She exits.*)

ROGER: Suit yourself, Annette. At the beginning of the day some of us enjoy our little peace.

CYRIL (*mutters*): Piss off.

MARION (*shocked*): Pardon, Cyril?

CYRIL (*smiles innocently*): Piece of sanity.

MARION (*nodding towards the open door*): Some chance with the whole school gawping in.

ROGER (*hotly*): All right, all right. I'm shutting the door. (*He goes over to the door, slams it in* MISS GRIMBLE's *face. She promptly opens it, pushing him out of the way.*) Sorry, Miss Grimble didn't see you there.

Enter BEA GRIMBLE.

BEA (*briskly*): Obviously. (*To the others.*) Morning all.

EVERYONE (*various versions of*): Good morning Miss Grimble.

BEA: Is Mrs Anderson here yet?

MARION: Not so far, Miss Grimble.

BEA: Bother.

LINDA (*helpfully*): It's very unusual. She must have got held up – the buses on Mondays are . . .

BEA: No matter, I'll try and catch her later on. (*She turns to go, then, as an afterthought:*) No more disgusting business in the toilets to report then, Miss Landsdowne?

MARION: Not as far as I am aware, Miss Grimble.

ROGER: Aye, aye, what's this then?

BEA (*coldly*): Since when have the girls' lavatories been your concern, Mr Cunningham?

ROGER (*weakly*): I beg your pardon.

Exit BEA GRIMBLE.

CYRIL: She was looking for Claire on Friday evening as well. Wonder what that's about.

ROGER: I'm more interested in Marion's revelations. (*To* MARION:) Come on, don't keep us guessing.

MARION: I'd have thought Miss Grimble made it quite plain that it was nothing for you to worry about.

ROGER: I'm sure you'll tell me at your own convenience. (*He laughs at his own joke, probably because nobody else does.*)

CYRIL: It's bad enough starting a new week without you cracking on like a crazed cockatoo, Cunningham. Give it a rest.

ROGER: Cyril, you are dry to the point of being wooden.

CYRIL: The rot has set in. What d'you expect? This place is a blight on my life.

MARION: Boys, boys.

Enter CLAIRE.

ROGER (*ever jocular*): Why, if it isn't Ms Anderson at last.

CLAIRE (*fake smile*): Master Cunningham, fancy seeing you here on time.

ROGER: And a bit ruffled you are too. Where have you been hiding him, down the leg of your dungarees?

In fact ROGER *has never seen* CLAIRE *wearing dungarees, but this fits his image of her.*

CLAIRE (*ignoring* ROGER): Morning, Linda, Marion, Cyril.

They respond appropriately.

ROGER: Our beloved Virgin Queen was looking for you.

CLAIRE: Typical, the very morning I'm late. What did she want?

ROGER: Didn't say but it's my bet I'm conversing with the next deputy headmistress.

CLAIRE: Don't talk rubbish.

Enter ANNETTE.

Morning Annette.

ANNETTE: Good morning, Mrs Anderson.

ROGER (*to* CLAIRE): Anyway she dropped a bombshell about some goings on in the girls' toilets and Marion was to abashed to enlighten me. I was wonderin if you could put me in the picture.

CLAIRE: I have no idea what you're talking about. Marion?

MARION: I found some graffiti last week

CLAIRE: Oh, that.

ROGER: Something juicy, I hope it was about me.

MARION: Hardly.

ROGER: Come on, then, you've got us a on the edge of our seats.

MARION (*embarrassed but trying to be nonchalant*): It was a phone number amongst other things . . . for a gay switchboard.

ANNETTE: That euphemism is quite disgusting. It's quite wrecked the poetry syllabus. Instead of being an expression of joy, it's an excuse for muffled titters. Who do you think wrote it?

MARION: More than likely one of the sixth form. There's some queer fish in your group, Claire.

CLAIRE: I wouldn't say that.

ROGER: Queer being the operative word. I was only thinking when Diane Collier came to the door that she was a bit butch.

ANNETTE: It doesn't bear thinking about.

CLAIRE (to ROGER): Just because she can see through you. In fact she's probably more intelligent than you.

CYRIL (to ROGER): That's not saying much.

MARION (to ANNETTE): I've always found her strange. Do you remember that campaign she started in the third year for girls to do metalwork? Luckily it was knocked on the head.

ANNETTE: Humm. She was so good at home economics, but had the audacity to tell me it was boring. At least I think that's what she meant by announcing it was creatively deflating.

CLAIRE: This is supposed to be the age of equality.

MARION: Whatever it's supposed to be, it's certainly not the age of perversity. Not in this school anyway. We must be on guard for hanky-panky or horseplay.

CLAIRE *picks up a copy of the* Daily Mirror, *which is on the table, and hides behind it.*

ANNETTE: You know, I saw a marvellous version of *Macbeth* a couple of years ago, with Peter O'Toole.

ROGER: Did you pay for him to accompany you?

ANNETTE (*coldly*): He was in it.

MARION: How wonderful.

ANNETTE: Roger, I'm sorry to say this but you make me ill.

MARION (*to* ANNETTE): Go on, dear.

ANNETTE: Mind, not that the blood wasn't ridiculously overdone.

ROGER: I bet you'd have preferred it medium-rare.

ANNETTE (*regardless*): But it brought a whole new perspective to the characters of the three witches, you know, a hint of, er, female intimacy . . . between them . . . which gave a real tinge of reality to their evilness.

CLAIRE'*s newspaper twitches.*

CYRIL (*with laboured consideration*): You know when I was at college –

ROGER: Shakespeare was still doing the rewrites.

CYRIL: Cunningham you are more stupid than most of the fourth form.

MARION: Just take no notice, Cyril.

CYRIL: We had an extraordinary woman in our year, trained to be a PE teacher – always wore men's clothes, rumour had it that she wore a truss on the hockey field.

On the words 'PE teacher' LINDA grabs a newspaper and hides behind it.

ROGER: You ever heard of pre-penile dementia, Cyril?

CYRIL: It's true.

ANNETTE: In any event, Marion's right, we better keep our eyes well-peeled.

The bell goes.

ROGER (*eagerly*): Unto the breach, dear friends, or fill the gap with our non-sexist teaching.

The others start to make a move. CLAIRE *puts the newspaper down.*

CLAIRE (*smiles*): I wish someone or something would fill that gap in your face.

ROGER: Ah ha, the pink maiden surfaces from under *The Mirror* – well read?

CLAIRE (*stonily*): What a big wit you are.

Scene Five

The same day. The staff room after school. Everyone except ROGER *is collecting books etc. to go home.*

ANNETTE: Miss Grimble's having a word with them now, before they go home.

MARION: Were they kissing on the lips?

ANNETTE: Yes.

ROGER: I presume you mean . . .

MARION: Mr Cunningham, you are obscene.

ANNETTE: I can quite believe it of the other one, but not Terri, I mean, she's quite attractive.

CYRIL: I don't believe it of Diane. Like I said, this woman at college wore men's clothes and when she played hockey . . .

ROGER: Just because one doesn't wear a codpiece does not necessarily mean avowed heterosexuality.

MARION: There just isn't anything natural about women kissing each other.

CLAIRE (*blurts out in spite of himself*): Oh yes, there is. (*Silence.*) I mean, er, there can be, for comfort, you know, at a funeral or such like.

ROGER: If I dropped dead, would you kiss Marion?

CLAIRE: If you dropped dead, I'd kiss everything in this school, including the dog shit in the playground.

ROGER: You'd do that for me. I'm so honoured.

ANNETTE: Spare us, Mrs Anderson, don't encourage him.

MARION: Ignore him. You know social intercourse only exites him.

LINDA: Anyway, I don't know what you're on about. I practically had to prize Terri off one of the boys from Drylands Park on the playing field this afternoon.

CYRIL: Could have been after his box.

LINDA: The cricket season hasn't started yet.

ROGER: How's that then, you've awakened our games mistress. Interesting to see who comes out to defend what. Next into bat, Mrs Anderson.

CLAIRE: I'm not defending anything. (*She starts to collect her stuff together.*)

LINDA: And I'm off home. Bye all.

Chorus of goodbyes. Exit LINDA.

ANNETTE: It's the parents I feel sorry for.

ROGER: Can't be very fruitful knowing there are bent genes in the family tree.

CYRIL: Luckily they can't reproduce themselves.

MARION: Public tolerance wouldn't trus them with the next generation.

ROGER: Some of them do have children though.

ANNETTE: Don't be ridiculous, how can they?

CYRIL: You'd be surprised, Annette, there are ways to get round anything these days.

ROGER: Even nature.

MARION: Not many ways round the unhappiness it must cause.

ROGER: I wouldn't worry, Marion, it on affects women who can't get men.

CLAIRE, *bag packed, coat over her arm is about to slink out.*

ANNETTE: Oh, Claire.

CLAIRE (*startled*): Yes? What?

ANNETTE: I'd almost forgotten. She wants to see you as well, before you go.

CLAIRE: Me? What for?

ANNETTE: I don't know. She didn't say

ROGER: Oh dear me, what are you teaching them, Mrs Anderson?

ANNETTE: Roger, I hate to say this, bu could you please shut your mouth?

ROGER: She'll probably want to see me next, with some winge about there not being enough *Romeo and Juliet* on the syllabus.

MARION: Rest assured, no one in their right mind would want to see you.

ROGER: Just let her try. I'll give her a ru for her money.

MARION: And if we're lucky, she'll give you your money and tell you to run. Ca give you a lift, Annette?

ANNETTE: Very kind of you, dear, goodnight everyone.

CYRIL: Come on, Cunningham, buy me drink down the pub.

ROGER: What? And miss the revelation

of Mrs Anderson's hush-hush rendezvous with our revered leader.

CLAIRE: I do not intend to be any longer than I have to. I'm going straight home after the confrontation.

ROGER: Oh go on, tell us, I'll wait.

CLAIRE: You'll be waiting a long time then, won't you? You know your problem, you're all id.

Exit CLAIRE.

ROGER: What's id?

CYRIL: Short for idiot.

Scene Six

The Headmistress's office. DIANE *and* TERRI *stand in front of the desk.* BEA GRIMBLE *sits behind it, fiddling with her fountain pen.*

BEA: This, as it appears to me, is a very serious matter. Would you care to offer any acceptable explanation?

TERRI (*spilling words in panic*): Yes, yes, it wasn't what you think at all. I was, er, like, just daydreaming about my boyfriend, with my eyes shut, you know how you do. Sorry, how one do . . . does?

BEA: No. Do enlighten me.

TERRI: A real good-looking, I mean, clever, intelligent, nice, very decent boy and Diane didn't see me and bumped into me by a mistake and we lost our balance, very silly, really.

BEA: Really. Is that a fact? Because it seems to me that maybe I should introduce school medicals, as everyone lolls round this place with their eyes shut. And tell me, Terri, do you often spend your days in the cloakroom, eyes closed, daydreaming about boys.

TERRI: Oh yes. I mean no. Although I've had hundreds of boyfriends but I'm going steady now with a boy, but I don't let it interfere with my school work.

BEA: I'm very pleased to hear it. What have you to say for yourself, Diane?

DIANE: Not a lot.

TERRI (*quickly*): It's true.

BEA: What is?

TERRI: What I've just said. She means she's got nothing to add.

BEA: You speak for Diane as well?

TERRI: No, no. I hardly know her.

BEA: I thought you were good friends.?

TERRI: Oh no, that was the third year, second year, well not even the first year. We were friends at primary school but we lost touch.

BEA: Until today.

TERRI: Yes, no, no, it was an accident, Miss Grimble, you know how clumsy adolescents are.

BEA: Indeed. (*Pause.*) Now, I must get this business straight. I'm sorry but I have to ask you, Terri: did you kiss Diane and umm, have you had an intimate relationship with her or anyone else for that matter?

TERRI (*almost shouts*): Men. (*Then:*) Men, er, boys and then not *intimate* intimate, but you know . . .

BEA: Thank you. That will do. And Diane, will you deign to tell us the truth about yourself.?

DIANE: I am a lesbian.

BEA (*quickly*): Terri, you may go.

TERRI *bolts for the door and exits, shutting it behind her.*

I beg your pardon.

DIANE (*slowly*): I said . . .

BEA: Thank you, that will do. What do you mean by walking in here and . . .

DIANE: But Miss Grimble, I know that hypocrisy is a value you don't encourage. Surely you didn't expect me to lie?

BEA: Just what would you have me encourage?

DIANE: I've never felt you would protect, let alone perpetuate prejudice.

BEA: As far as awareness goes I'm taken to be a leading light in this authority, but I don't need to remind you that we are very much stuck in a backwater – though whether this would be tolerated anywhere is doubtful. (*Firmly:*) Now, as long as you keep your private life to yourself, and the subject is never, I repeat, never mentioned in this establishment again – you can go.

DIANE: It's what I am, it's not a hobby that I can keep shut up in an attic, even if I wanted to.

BEA (*controlled*): You will keep quiet. Do you hear me?

DIANE: If I don't say it, who will? We are nowhere in history books, sex education leaves us out, the media makes us into gross caricatures, when society does recognise us, it's only to oppress and . . .

BEA (*the voice of generous authority*): Diane, while it is between you and I, I am prepared to let the matter rest, but once a name is put on it publicly it will involve condemnation from staff, parents and pupils alike. And once the education authority get wind, it could affect the whole community.

DIANE (defiantly): That's not my problem.

Pause.

BEA: In that case you'll have to be transferred.

DIANE: I won't.

BEA: I'm sure you need no reminding that I am the headmistress of this school, not the inspectorate of people's preference of partner. You will do as I say or leave.

DIANE: But I'm in the middle of my mocks.

BEA: You should have thought of that before you tried to make a travesty of me. Get out of my sight.

DIANE: But . . .

BEA: NOW!

DIANE *exits to find* TERRI *outside.*

TERRI: What happened?

DIANE (*snaps*): Well, I didn't win no luxury cruise to Lesbos.

TERRI: I don't suppose you did, fancy coming out with it like that. What happened to what we agreed to say?

DIANE: I didn't agree to say anything.

TERRI: You said to me to say what I felt best saying.

DIANE: You felt best coming out with all that?!

TERRI: The point is, I got away with it, didn't I? Couldn't you see that old Bea was prepared to accept anything but the truth? Rudest word she's ever heard is pantie-girdle.

DIANE: And that makes you feel better getting away with what? A load of silly lies.

TERRI (*angry*): Well, I hope you're able to come up with a stronger word than silly because when the others find out, our lives will be hell.

DIANE: That remains to be seen.

TERRI: So all you've proved is that you've got more courage than me. (*She half turns.*)

DIANE: Look, I didn't mean . . .

TERRI: No, and you didn't have to either. (*She exits.*)

DIANE: Terri? (*She goes after her and bumps into* CLAIRE.)

CLAIRE: Hello, Diane, what's happened?

DIANE (*nods towards* BEA's *office*): She reckons I've got to leave.

CLAIRE (*shocked*): Leave?

DIANE: Can you try and explain to her?

CLAIRE: I'm not sure . . .

DIANE (*flatly*): No, I didn't think you would be.

Exit DIANE. CLAIRE *knocks on the door.*

BEA: Come.

CLAIRE *enters the office.* BEA *has tried to regain her air of authoritative calm.*

CLAIRE (*tense*): You wanted to see me, Miss Grimble.

BEA: Ah, Mrs Anderson, do take a pew. I expect you have an inkling as to why I asked you here.

CLAIRE: Well, I . . .

BEA: I did try and get hold of you this morning but you were rather elusive.

CLAIRE: I'm sorry I was late.

BEA: No matter. I have spoken to Mr

Graham at EO6.

CLAIRE: But I was only a few minutes late. I was here by the bell.

BEA: No, no, that is of no consequence. Mr Graham was most understanding, although it's slightly unusual. As from this week I'd like to appoint you as acting deputy head.

CLAIRE: Do what? I mean, pardon?

BEA: With an honorarium to your salary of course.

CLAIRE: I'm sorry. I mean, what a surprise.

BEA: I know you're young but your qualifications are first class, literally, and you're a very popular member of this establishment with staff and pupils alike.

CLAIRE: Thanks. Err . . . thank you. Thank you very much indeed. It's a great honour.

BEA: If you'll forgive me for saying so, you look quite perplexed. What did you think I was going to say?

CLAIRE: I thought it was about Diane Collier.

BEA: Oh, that wretched child. It's too despicable for words. I've been on to St Saviour's only they won't take her. They say they've got enough sexual perverts without starting a trend with the girls.

CLAIRE: But . . . (*Carefully.*) I mean . . . with all due respect, isn't that a bit drastic?

BEA: Drastic, no, I don't think so. Heavens, you're not condoning the girl? (*Then:*) Are you?

CLAIRE: Heavens, no, (*Beat.*) no, (*Beat.*) no. It's just that she's very clever.

BEA: Too damn bad. She's got to go.

CLAIRE: But forcing her to go isn't very good publicity.

BEA: It doesn't bode too well, I agree. Now, as acting deputy head, have you got any better suggestions?

BEA: It did occur to me that maybe, if she agreed to see an Ed. Psych.

BEA: Excellent, excellent. I'll call Mr Forthingay.

CLAIRE: No. I mean, I know he's very good.

BEA (*nods*): Knows his stuff.

CLAIRE: But I'm thinking of one who specialises in this sort of thing.

BEA: What's his name?

CLAIRE: Jean, Jean Boyd. She's a woman.

BEA (*disappointed*): Oh.

CLAIRE (*hopefully*): She's got a PhD.

BEA: Very well, I'll leave it in your capable hands and I'll announce your appointment in assembly tomorrow.

CLAIRE: Thank you, Miss Grimble.

CLAIRE *leaves the office, shutting the door behind her, and bumps into* ROGER.

ROGER: So what did she want?

CLAIRE: You'll know soon enough.

ROGER: Go on, you can tell me.

CLAIRE: Go away. (*She starts to walk,* ROGER *trying to keep up with her.*)

ROGER: Luckily I have more appeal for my students.

CLAIRE: Because your disicipline is atrocious.

ROGER: I encourage them subtly, of course, to feel good about themselves.

CLAIRE: Huh, subtlety is an adjective that has escaped your description for the best part of your life.

ROGER: Like today I complimented them by telling them that one of the rewards of teaching A level English was that it attracted mostly girls. Unfortunately in my position it's like looking at a box of chocolates when you're on a diet.

CLAIRE: I hope they reported you.

ROGER: They loved it. Giggles and blushes all round. Had them eating out of my hand. Except that Diane Whatsit girl. D'you want a lift home?

CLAIRE: No, just get out of my way.

209312

Scene Seven

Monday evening. POPPY and JEAN are in the living-room. Enter CLAIRE.

POPPY: When she comes in I'm going to give her the biggest hug and kiss. Mum. (*She rushes to meet her. CLAIRE picks her up and kisses her.*)

CLAIRE: How was school?

POPPY: Horrible. I got told off again for talking and our teacher told us a story about Jesus being nailed to a cross and I said if that was on a film on telly my mum wouldn't let me watch it. But d'you know what? She wanted us to draw a picture of it.

CLAIRE: Oh. What did she say?

POPPY: She said, next time I wanted to butt in, I was to put my hand up.

CLAIRE (*nods*): Uh huh.

POPPY: So I did.

CLAIRE: Oh?

POPPY: I had to. You know what she said next? That Jesus forgave the robbers and muggers that were hanging round him and they went to heaven.

CLAIRE (*shrugs*): That's how the story goes.

POPPY: I said, if someone mugged my nan I wouldn't forgive them and my nan would be really mad if they ended up in heaven with her. She would, wouldn't she?

CLAIRE: What did Miss Stokes say to that?

POPPY: Get on and draw your picture. And guess what? Tony Sudenham did one of Jesus and used real blood.

CLAIRE (*shocked*): Whose?

POPPY: He cut his knee at playtime and there was enough for the hands. Show off. Huh, he cried when he fell over, though. The boys mostly did muggers with tattoos but our table didn't. What did you do today?

CLAIRE: Well, I got made acting deputy head.

JEAN looks up from the book she's reading.

JEAN: That's fantastic, well done.

POPPY: Brillo, Mum. Now you can boss everyone about.

CLAIRE: Not quite.

POPPY (*jumps up*): I forgot, I forgot. I made a present for you. Wait there. (*She exits.*)

CLAIRE: Thanks for collecting her for me.

JEAN: It's no trouble especially as your meeting with Miss Grimble proved fruitful. That's great news, Claire, couldn't be better.

CLAIRE: Unfortunately, one small cloud on the horizon. Diane came out today . . .

JEAN: Can't you tactfully shut the closet door before she gets flushed away altogether.

CLAIRE: In style in the headmistress's office whilst the headmistress was still in there.

JEAN: What is it they say, better latent than never?

CLAIRE: Really, Jean, that's a Roger Cunningham remark!

JEAN: Sorry, mind, it's a great idea for updating a Bessie Bunter story.

CLAIRE: Beatrix the matrix wants her transferred to St Saviour's.

JEAN: St Saviour's??!

CLAIRE: Only they won't take her.

JEAN: If she's in the sixth form she could leave.

CLAIRE: But she stands to get at least two A levels.

JEAN: Oh, how we cling to academia.

CLAIRE: I suggested that we get an Ed. Psych. in.

JEAN: Are you mad? They're all a bunch of wankers.

CLAIRE: Not just any Ed. Psych.

JEAN: Oh, I'm with you. It's okay by me.

CLAIRE: You know, just nod and mutter a few clichés.

JEAN (*agreeing*): Yes, some large fib about if a fuss is made of this at this stage it could be habit-forming.

CLAIRE: That's it, that sort of thing.

JEAN: Talking of which, I hope you didn't betray yourself.

CLAIRE (*flatly*): Throughout the day I invalidated myself three times. If that's what you mean.

JEAN: And a cock crowed thrice?

CLAIRE: Roger Cunningham visibly preened himself but his feathers will soon ruffle when he hears of my promotion.

Re-enter POPPY *with a large piece of paper, rolled up, in one hand, and a book in the other.*

POPPY: Here it is. (*Unrolling the paper.*) It's a picture of a woman holding the world still.

CLAIRE: Poppy, it's lovely. Thank you. We'll put it on the wall.

POPPY: Mum, would it be okay if Sharon comes round tonight?

CLAIRE: Yes, I should think so.

Doorbell.

POPPY: That'll be her. (*She rushes to the door.*)

CLAIRE (*laughs*): Just as well I said yes.

POPPY (*off*): Hello Nan, hello Sharon. Mum's in there.

JOYCE: Thank you, Poppy.

JEAN *and* CLAIRE *exchange glances.* JEAN *gets up as* JOYCE *enters.*

There you are. (She sees JEAN.) Oh hello . . .

JEAN (*nods*): Joyce.

JOYCE: That's funny, that's my name too.

JEAN: I know, hello Joyce, my name's Jean.

JOYCE: Oh yes, sorry Jean. You know a friend of Poppy's walked up the street with me.

CLAIRE: Oh, that's Sharon.

JOYCE: She looked at me like I was off the telly and said, hey, are you Poppy's nan? Like I was wonderful or something.

CLAIRE (*teasing*): You're complaining about that?

JOYCE: I just wonder what the child has

told her, any rate, that's not the point.

CLAIRE: Do you want a cuppa tea?

JOYCE: I didn't come all the way over here to have a cup of tea, did I? That's what you think of me, shut the old girl up with a cup of tea.

CLAIRE: Sorry.

JOYCE: I know. I know. But I've been stewing on it all day. Colin had a quiet word with me yesterday and he's so worried about Val. He asked me if I'd pop round this evening because he has to work late but we're not to let on to Val.

CLAIRE: We?

JOYCE: You get on with her so much better than me. It's just a feeling; I don't know – you know what they're like these medical people – love drama – take you away in the middle of the night, so if you weren't disorientated in the first place, you soon will be, waking up in an ambulance at two in the morning.

CLAIRE: They won't be able to take Val to hospital if she doesn't want to go.

JOYCE: She just seems to have let go of herself. Please, Claire?

JEAN: Don't worry, I'll see that Sharon gets home all right.

CLAIRE: Okay, Mum, I'll come with you. I'll get my coat and tell Poppy where I'm going.

JOYCE: Thanks. (*Exit* CLAIRE. *Silence.*) Claire told me you're one of these psychological people. What do you think about our Val?

JEAN: I don't really know her, but from what I can see, I think she's just unhappy.

JOYCE: Humph. Well, happiness doesn't grow on trees.

JEAN: Nor does powerlessness.

Enter CLAIRE *with her coat on.*

CLAIRE: Come on, I'm ready.

Scene Eight

VAL's *living room.* VAL, COLIN, SID JNR *and* WALTER.

COLIN: Right, shall I put these two to bed

before I pop out?

VAL (*shakes her head*): No.

COLIN: Don't worry, I'll only be twenty minutes at most. I'm sorry, I've got to get this paperwork back to Tim, it won't wait until the morning. You wouldn't believe how hectic things are at the office. All of a sudden Easter holidays have become very popular.

VAL (*flatly, quietly*): You don't have to spy on me.

COLIN: Val, please . . . love, don't give in to those ideas. (VAL *turns away.*) Believe me, I only want what's best, really. Anything, Val . . . I'd do anything to get you back to your old self. (VAL *nods.*) I'm just at a loss as to what to do. Are you sure you'll be all right . . . you only have to say.

VAL (*nods*): You go.

COLIN: Like I say, I won't be long. Okay, I'm going. (*He puts on a jacket.*) Now Walter, Sid, behave yourselves until Daddy gets back. (*He kisses* VAL *and exits.*)

COLIN *has left his briefcase behind.*

SID: I'm a condor.

WALTER: I'm a condor.

Both play aeroplanes, making appropriate noises, running round the settee on which VAL *sits.*

WALTER: Mummy, play. Control over. Come in. Over, over.

SID: Control. Tower come in. Mummy! Come in! Mummy!

VAL *lies on the settee.*

WALTER (*shakes her gently*): Mum, you are the control tower.

SID: She's not.

WALTER: Mummy no good.

SID: Come on. Nice Mum.

WALTER: Sleep. No good.

SID: Mummy runway.

WALTER: Yeah, Mummy play.

They both run round the settee. Then one at a time crawl over VAL, *stand on the arm of the settee and jump off. They are*

about to do it for a second time when VAL *grabs* WALTER, *not viciously, and sits him on the floor. In the tussle a glass of orange juice gets knocked over.* WALTER *isn't hurt but shocked, wailing*

Ahh, Mummy, ahhhhhhhh, it hurts, it hurts.

SID: Orange gone. Broken. Mummy. (*He starts wailing.*)

Both continue to cry. VAL, *helpless, sits, vaguely stroking their hair.* SID *looks at the glass.*

Orange gone.

WALTER: Get nother one.

SID: Play boats, play boats.

WALTER: Yeah.

They both exit to the kitchen. The sound of a scraping chair as they drag it across to the sink and then the sound of a tap running. COLIN *re-enters.*

COLIN: Forgot the sodding papers, didn't I? (*He picks up his briefcase but is torn by the sight of* VAL.) Val, love, please just talk to me. I don't know what to do, can't you see how much I love you?

VAL: I don't want to take responsibility for this relationship any longer.

COLIN (*gently*): Val, I don't know what you mean. I don't come from a home, a place where relationships were discussed. If anything was wrong something got broken after a lot of shouting, I understand that. How do you expect me to cope with this? No one ever taught me what to do or how to behave, let alone how to respond, it's not the sort of thing that ever gets mentioned in schools. What's the use of knowing that Barnes Wallis invented the bouncing bomb or what SALT stands for, or remembering the French for grapefruit when you've never ever been to France. And nothing, if I could remember it all, nothing would be of help, I learnt nothing that I could apply to my life. (*Pause.*) I love you because you're strong. I never wanted a woman at home who was little more than a servant because that's all my dad knew of marriage. I don't want a wife, not in that sense, but I want you, Val, you, you and the boys – you're all I've got. I'm so proud of you. I want to make this work.

Just tell me what to do and I will try. Honest to God, Val, I need you. Can't you . . .

He turns.

Oh hell . . .

He gets up. Exit COLIN.
   After a long pause, VAL *gets up. She goes over to the window and smashes her fists and arms through it. The sound of breaking glass prompts* COLIN *to re-enter.*

Christ Almighty. Val. Oh God. (*He crosses to her. Then, gently:*) Now, let's have a look, come on, put your hand over, we've got to stop the blood. Oh why love? (*Looking round frantically for a bandage.*) Where's the plasters? Oh Val, have we got any bandages? (*Opening and shutting drawers.*) I knew we should have bought that first-aid kit when we saw it in Argos. (*He takes off his jacket and shirt and proceeds to wrap the shirt around* VAL's *arm.*) There, sorry, sorry, come on, we'll have to get it seen to . . . Where are . . . Sid? Walter? (*He exits to the kitchen.*) Get off the table. What did you tell them to do, flood the place? (*He re-enters with* SID *and* WALTER.) Come on, you two get in the car. (*He steers* VAL *with his arm.*) Come on, love. Why? Oh Why?

SID: Where we going? Where we going?

WALTER: Mummy mummy.

Enter CLAIRE *and* JOY[...] *front door which* COLIN [...]

CLAIRE: Sorry, we did kn[...] what's happened?

COLIN: At last. Thank Go[...] you come earlier?

JOYCE: Val, what have you [...] she done to her arm, what [...] happened. Colin, what . .

COLIN (*nods to the window* [...] herself. Please could you t[...] and look after the boys.

JOYCE: I'll come with you.

COLIN: Please.

CLAIRE: We'll stay here, M[...] least put your jacket on. N[...] look.

COLIN (*feeling his bare chest*): Oh God. (*Putting on his jacket.*) Don't touch that, she's losing blood.

CLAIRE (*swiftly takes the sleeve off the shirt, redoes the bandage so it's tighter*): It's not that bad, it will need stitches though, Val.

COLIN: Please I must get her to hospital.

JOYCE: You're not going to let her stay in hospital, are you? Colin, answer me, are you?

COLIN: I'm not going to have her bleed to death on the carpet.

JOYCE: I'm coming with you.

CLAIRE: No, Mum.

COLIN: No. Stay here. (*He propels* VAL *through the door. They exit.*)

JOYCE (*shouts after him*): Don't you dare let them do anything but sew the arm up.

SID: Mummy gone. (*He starts to cry.*)

WALTER: Daddy gone. (*He starts to cry.*)

CLAIRE: Only for a little while. They'll be back soon. Come on, come here for a cuddle.

CLAIRE *cuddles* WALTER; JOYCE *cuddles* SID.

JOYCE (*feeling* SID's *feet*): Their shoes and socks are wringing wet. Poor loves. (*She gets up, finds a towel and dries their feet. She puts clean socks o[...] n stuffs*

[handwritten: New Book Shelf]

[...] wrists?

[...] e arm.

[...]'s the
[...] m. I'll
[...] a story.
[...] less.
[...] til Colin
[...] y and do
[...] LTER.
[...] low up,
[...] LAIRE

can't hear her.

I was in Woolworth's the other day. You wouldn't remember when nothing in there was over sixpence. It seemed like magic when I was a child. Until I was caught stealing a bar of chocolate and tasted nothing but humiliation. Mind, it's all changed now, but what hasn't? I don't think they can have any store-rooms in Woolies, you know, because it seems that all the stock is on the shelves. Rows and rows of the same thing but some of them are still good value. Any rate, I was just comparing the price of the wrap and seal bags when but a few feet away this man went off his nut. I was going to say 'off his trolley' but you might have got confused with shopping trolley and thought I was going to have a dig at the way men don't seem to be in control of the things, let alone what they buy. Do you know that most wives have to write the shopping list in order in accordance to how you go around the shop otherwise you can find a pile up round the poultry. All it takes is for one of them to be a vegetarian and it needs the assistant manager and a pair of wire cutters to de-mesh them. Anyhow, that's beside the point – this chap didn't even have a basket. He was just stood there standing and he blew a gasket. Flipped. Shouting and screaming words what nobody could make out but sounded like something like 'Alley Waly Gumbroil' and he started smashing his fist over and over the massive piles of soaps so there were bars of Lux, Fairy Toilet, Shield, Imperial Leather – you name it, flying all over the shop. Literally. It was quite a few moments before he was apprehended and, as he launched attack after attack into what was left of the display, so even the plastic price labels attached to the chrome racks started pinging from place to place. I caught myself thinking: let them punch soap all over the show as long as they don't hit their wives.

Not that any of you have ever been hit by a man, to my knowledge anyway. Colin is such a lamb, isn't he? And it wasn't so long ago that our Val thought God's grand plan meant a Shreiber fitted kitchen. As for Lawrence, he was nothing like he is now. D'you remember he used to wear so many badges that when I saw him without them his shirt had so many

perforations I nearly dunked him in a cup of boiling water. Yes, like a teabag it was. Oh, and in the winter he wore those silly loud jumpers with reindeer prancing all over them. Talk about migraine, I tell you, Claire, you was lucky to get away without a brain tumour. Not that I was a hundred per cent, to say the least, behind you leaving him like that, it must have been a real blow to his do-da. But well, before that, mind, he used to make quite an effort to get on with me. Clever that, because I know you're not supposed to have favourites and I treat them all the same – you were always special to me. So he knew what he was doing when you first started going out together. My instinct is to say courting but you all cringe and say, 'Aw Mum, no one says courting these days.' Well, my vocabulary has had a lot of new words prised into it over the years and you have to be careful because there's a lot of difference between 'going out' and 'coming out'. I tell you sometimes, I get so tongue-tied I don't know whether – but what's that to do with anything. Nothing. Where was I? Oh yes, so he had me sussed out, as they say. Invited me to his bachelor pad for Sunday tea. He apologised for the state of it. Apparently there'd been a party the night before. It was a bit messy and he must have noticed that I was almost wearing myself out sitting still while the hoover lay dormant. So by way of distraction, he told me that someone had arrived with a bottle of sherry which had been made in South Africa and as a matter of principle he'd poured it down the sink. Myself, I couldn't help thinking it was a pity Vim wasn't made in South Africa. His family was worth a bob or two, I can tell you. Well, you could tell for yourself they went to the theatre practically every other week and that, but him, he had no time for it, turned his back and shunned the lot of them, and he was always raving on to me about authentic working-class culture – whatever that is when it's at home. I'd supposed he meant the group of fire-eaters on stilts who blocked the pavement, outside the Town Hall, when Nalgo were on strike.

We are talking about a man who used to call coppers pigs, the Beak – right-wing scum, and the law – by that I mean the legal system the whole shebang – 'a heap of shite'. But being who he is he can use it anyway he wants because that's what it's there for and I should know, amount of times he told me.

Not that this turncoat soft-peddling didn't eat at him, because it did. He took his contrary ideas and guilt and inflicted them on a therapist. Didn't last long though. He told me, while I was still speaking to him that is, why he'd jacked it in. 'Huh,' I said to him, I said, 'Lawrence, it's a fine to-do, in this day and age when the ultimate in humiliation for a grown man like yourself is when your therapist yawns at you.'

Enter CLAIRE, *not having heard a word coherently.*

CLAIRE (*impatiently*): Mum, can you keep the noise down. They're asleep.

JOYCE: I'll never understand what came over you. He wasn't such a bad bloke. He might have had some weird ideas but then, let's face it, he wasn't the only one.

CLAIRE (*angrily*): For Christ's sake don't start all that up now!

Scene Nine

Friday morning. Staff room. Breaktime.
ROGER *eating a packet of crisps. Enter* CLAIRE.

ROGER: Good morning, deputy éclaire, our matriarch's mentor and minion.

CLAIRE: Mr Cunningham, as acting deputy head, I must remind you of your place which, were it not for the advantages awarded to the unfairer sex, would be down a lavatory pan.

ROGER: What a superb metaphor. Ms Anderson, one may venture even for you Milton has not lost his use.

CLAIRE: Indeed he hasn't, I sincerely hope you take after him. (*She drops the book,* The Complete Works of Milton, *which* ROGER *has open on a table.*) Go blind and wank yourself into oblivion.

ROGER: Fortunately, my paradise isn't lost to a loud-mouthed . . .

CLAIRE: Language, sir, language, we simply cannot tolerate your hot hyperboles in this school.

ROGER *is stopped from shouting any*

further adjectives by MARION *entering, followed by* ANNETTE.

CLAIRE (*about to walk past them, to* ROGER): Have a nice day.

MARION: Claire, Claire, have you seen this? (*Brandishing a copy of the school magazine.*)

Enter LINDA.

CLAIRE (*to* MARION): No. (*To* LINDA:) Hello, Linda, how's things?

LINDA (*looking at* MARION): Fine.

CLAIRE *shows no interest in the magazine and* ROGER *takes it from* MARION.

MARION: Liberal teaching methods are to blame. They can't say I didn't warn them.

LINDA: Don't go overboard, Marion, it's simply the agitation of one girl.

MARION: Girl? If you can call her a girl. I'm not aware of any pronouns for neuters. Actually, I supposed you'd be the best person to ask about that, Roger.

ROGER (*looks up, offended*): Just what do you mean by that?

MARION: Is there another pronoun other than he or she?

ROGER: 'It' – no man's land.

MARION: Quite.

ROGER: Anyway, if you'll excuse me. I can't stand here all day discussing the ins and outs of hermaphrodites.

MARION: No, you can't, Miss Grimble's coming.

ROGER: Don't get excited, Marion, she always makes that noise – it's chronic bronchitis. (MARION *looks confused.* LINDA *and* CLAIRE *act as though no one is in the room. A little louder; he continues for the sake of talking really:*) What do you call a shiny receptacle from which ale is poured from a great height? – Beer Tricks Thimble.

Enter BEA GRIMBLE *with* CYRIL *in tow. She gives* ROGER *a withering look.*

CYRIL (*as they enter is muttering to* BEA, *who is totally oblivious of him*): And rumour has it, when on the rugger field.

BEA: Please take a seat, I want a word with

you all. Don't worry, Miss Pollard is with the sixth form. This is a very serious matter. Ah, Mrs Anderson, would you sit here next to me. (MARION *is forced to change places with* CLAIRE.) Thank you, I'm sorry I've not had time to discuss this with you personally, Claire, but in view of the urgency of the matter, I'm sure you'll understand. Now, have you all seen a copy of the school end-of-term magazine?

MARION: I have, Miss Grimble.

BEA: In view of the fact that I've forgotten my reading glasses amidst the fracas, would you care to read for us?

MARION (*quickly*): No, I would not. (*A look from* BEA.) I couldn't, I couldn't possibly. I mean its sentiment is completely beyond my comprehension.

BEA: Quite likely. Very well. (*She looks at* CLAIRE.)

CLAIRE (*reluctantly*): I'll read it.

BEA: Thank you. (*She hands them all a copy.*) Back page.

CLAIRE: From here?

BEA: Yes. (*She sighs.*) It's not really the sports fixtures that concern us today. (*She nods to* CLAIRE.) Thank you.

CLAIRE (*reads*): Women should never again have to apologise for loving each other. How natural is it to spend your life in service to a man? When I deny through silence I am only reinforcing my isolation. I am a lesbian and I am not alone.

Silence, during which CLAIRE *does not look up.*

BEA (*almost sadly*): I don't think it's too hard to nail down the author of that. There is, however, another piece in the third person. Perhaps we should hear that?

She nods to CLAIRE *but* CLAIRE *passes the magazine to* MARION *who is left with little choice other than to read it.*

MARION (*reads*): It is about time the education system recognised the hypocrisy it transmits while trying to be liberal in its purporting to care for the individual. Its liberalism is total reactionary rubbish and sexist crap. We are not allowed freedom of choice over our sexuality, which if it is different to that as suggested by the hierarchy of this establishment, is evil. We have a right to our identity and we are not going to be silenced by a smack in the gob from this fascist, poxy school.

ROGER (*stifles a laugh*): That's told us.

BEA: You'll be laughing on the other side of your face if I find the culprits, who obviously can't string a sentence together to be in your English A level group. (*Silence.*) Yes, it renders me speechless, what do you make of it, Mrs Anderson?

CLAIRE: I agree, the syntax is foul.

BEA: Is that all you have to say?

CLAIRE: No. (*Slight pause.*) I mean . . . it's dreadful, disgraceful, disgusting.

MARION: I don't understand how it got there.

BEA: Someone or something obviously typed it on to the last stencil and put it back in the pile awaiting duplicating and collating. Although how they obtained the key will, I suppose, remain a mystery.

MARION: Ah, Miss Evans has been off and . . .

BEA: Miss Evans's attendance or lack of it in this school is not the topic under discussion, that is a matter for this evening's board of governors meeting. But this (*Jabbing at the article with her finger.*) business must on no account be allowed to get that far. Which is why we are thrashing it out now. Perhaps Mr Cunningham is the best person to enlighten us as to the precise, punctuation aside, meaning of the wording.

ROGER (*studying the wording*): Educational, i.e. learning.

BEA: Don't try and be funny, Mr Cunningham. This is not a merry jape. I am quite aware of the connotations of 'educational', 'hypocrisy', 'sexuality' and 'rubbish'. Neither do I need David Owen to point out the connections between 'liberalism', 'reactionary' and 'fascism'. I am stumbling over poxy.

ROGER: Ah, it's . . . the clap.

BEA: And what's that when it's at home, a new wave dance step?

ROGER: Venereal disease.

BEA: God help us all. Is that rife, as well? It would seem that this institution is nothing but a hotbed of perverted promiscuity.

CYRIL (*thoughtfully, matter of factly*): Rest assured, Beatrice, it is impossible for women to transmit syphilis to one another. The germ can only breed in the heat created by the friction of the erect penis in the vagina.

BEA (*looks as though she might be sick*): Spare us, please.

MARION (*shocked*): Cyril, I thought your degree was in physics.

CYRIL: I am qualified to teach biology, only I always considered it more of a woman's subject.

BEA (*recovered*): Indeed. Thank you, Mr Barrett.

CYRIL: My blood pressure runs amok at the thought of teaching fifth form girls the ups and downs of menstrual cycles.

BEA (*firmly, singsong*): Thank you.

ROGER: On your bike, Cyril.

BEA (*raising her voice*): Mr Cunningham.

ROGER: Poxy, Miss Grimble, is used as an expletive, a swear word. Obviously, the authors or authoresses do not hold the school in very high regard.

BEA: Obviously. (*Slight pause.*) Mrs Anderson came up with an excellent formula for negotiation but it has gone too far for us to put it into operation.

CYRIL: They must be helped in some way, surely.

MARION: I don't know about that – it must be stamped out, this sort of thing breeds like wildfire.

BEA: What do you suggest?

MARION: For what?

BEA: For those who fly in the face of the fabric of society.

CLAIRE: I know it goes against . . .

MARION: It goes against everything decent people hold dear.

CLAIRE: Such as?

CYRIL: God and the family. To name but

everything in two.

BEA: Not that the nuclear physics goes against God and the family, I don't suppose, Mr Barrett?

ROGER: Never mind the Holy Trinity. Marion's right, if this thing doesn't get hushed up there's no telling what will happen. It's a real threat to the other girls.

LINDA (*everyone including herself is shocked at this outburst*): You think so? You really think so? You think the possibility so attractive to girls in this school, let alone society, that they will relinquish the security of friends and family? Are you really suggesting that the possibility is so viable that they, with nothing less than gay abandon, will shrug off all social pressures and become outcasts? (*Stunned silence, then half-mumbled:*) Although if they all did they wouldn't be outcasts . . .

MARION: Which is why it mustn't be allowed to get to that.

CYRIL: Oh God, we'll have the papers round here, none of us can handle that.

ROGER: Why should we? This would never happen in a mixed school. I've always said it was unhealthy.

BEA: There is nothing healthy about girls failing, Mr Cunningham.

ROGER: That's as maybe, but you felt the need to appoint male staff.

BEA: On the contrary, it wasn't me, it was the poxy Equality of Opportunities Commission.

ROGER: Oh.

BEA: None of this is solving our dilemma. I want you all to send every girl in the school who could possibly be a (*Slight pause.*) whatever, if you follow my drift, to me.

CLAIRE: With all due respect, Miss Grimble, that could implicate all the girls in the school.

BEA: I hardly think so.

LINDA: It might be just the one girl. We don't actually know that there's more.

BEA: We cannot afford to take that chance my dear. There is definitely more than one style of writing and too many leaks can sink the ship.

MARION: We don't know who'll get hold of this. (*Brandishing the magazine.*) Anyone could read it.

BEA: Precisely. That's why those responsible must somehow be rounded up and be seen to be punished.

MARION: I suppose if they mean what they say they'll become visible to us. I mean hold a meeting. Shouldn't be hard to find them.

BEA: Good. Good. Thank you, Miss Landsdowne. With a bit of luck we'll be shot of this matter before the end of term. From now until then I'd be very grateful if we could have all hands on deck. Anything suspicious, send them to me. (*She gets up*). Is that clear?

Various responses of 'Yes' with varying degrees of enthusiasm. BEA GRIMBLE crosses to the door and opens it.

ROGER (*mutters*): What a gay day.

BEA (*turns*): Mr Cunningham, you are provoking me beyond the pale. (*Parting shot.*) Humm, poxy? Old-fashioned words for me are just as sufficient. Nincompoop seems to fit the bill adequately in your case.

She exits.

CYRIL (*gets up and stumbles after BEA, mumbling*): Miss Grimble, if I could have a word with you about the blocked Bunsens.

CLAIRE (*more to herself than anyone in particular*): I just don't believe this.

MARION: Miss Grimble's right, though, this matter's got out of hand.

ROGER: Or in hand, depending on how you see it.

MARION: It's a good job Annette isn't here, as she'd be sorry to have to say how you make her feel.

ROGER: Huh, well, what a good thing we haven't got an Easter pantomime. The poor creature playing Mary Magdalene would well and truly be in the spotlight.

MARION: Don't be stupid. Anyway she was always washing our Lord's feet.

ROGER (*mimicking BEA GRIMBLE*): Oh, Miss Landsdowne, don't tell me foo fetishes are rife as well? I'm so pleased to see you're not taking this lying down. Come along now, ladies, time to get you fingers out. (*He laughs and exits.*)

MARION: Shame he couldn't marry Miss Evans and catch whatever it is she's got.

LINDA: The shame of it is that it couldn't be terminal.

MARION: Really now, Linda, that's nasty. I wouldn't wish that on anyone. (*She looks at her watch.*) I could put the couple of minutes before the bell to worse use than a quick cruise round the sixth hangouts. (*She exits.*)

CLAIRE (*still holding the magazine*): Wha am I going to do?

LINDA: Don't look at me.

CLAIRE: Not unless there was a hundred per cent rebellion and every girl in the school said she was gay.

LINDA: Could you have agreed to that when you were their age?

CLAIRE: No. The only common denominator is silence.

LINDA: I don't know how you can say tha with this screaming up at you. (*She takes the magazine from CLAIRE and drops it on the table.*)

Scene Ten

Hospital day room. VAL sits in a chair doing the crossword. Enter CLAIRE.

CLAIRE: Hi.

VAL: Not particularly.

CLAIRE: Sorry.

VAL: Take no notice. If madder only had one 'd' it would be an anagram of dream

CLAIRE: Armed with unfulfilled ones.

VAL: Something like that. (*She puts the paper down.*) What about you?

CLAIRE: Oh, all right. (*Pause.*) Well, I might have been if one of the girls hadn't come out at school; that could have been copeable-with only, to that headcase of a man I had the misjudgement to marry, getting married means that nothing stands in his way of getting Poppy, even though he never bothered to see her for three years, even though he's unreliable about access now, that matters nothing except of course that I will be forced through a farce which masquerades as justice. It wouldn't be so bad if an article hadn't appeared in the school magazine, which apart from repercussions to my job (*She stops herself.*) Sorry, Gawd, listen to me. Maybe you and I should swop places.

VAL: Maybe we're in the same boat.

CLAIRE: Here I am trying to prove what a normal mother I am.

VAL (*raising her voice*): Where are the 'normals'?

CLAIRE: Shush, keep your voice down.

VAL: Where are they, this invisible minority who can put their hands together and thank God every morning that they were born one of the great, white, washed normals?

CLAIRE: They sit in judgement, perched on benches, tightly permed, decaying wigs balanced on their heads. Looking like ten-stone owls.

VAL: If it wasn't so serious it would be ludicrous.

CLAIRE: We seem to be caught in a horrendous fairy-tale.

VAL: Huh, that's true, the doctors in here are clones of the Brothers Grimm. Mum tells me you and her had words.

CLAIRE: Words, huh. Screams more like. We had a furious row. What did she go and bother you with that for?

VAL: Because she's afraid for you.

CLAIRE: Well, she should try and do something about it instead of finding fault all the time.

VAL: You know, you were always her favourite.

CLAIRE: Rubbish. I'm the scapegoat. She just launched into why didn't I stay with Lawrence and God knows what.

VAL: Well, I've asked her to bring some make-up in for me.

CLAIRE: Oh?

VAL (*with irony*): Seems that you get on better in here if you spend an hour in front of the mirror each morning. And Mum was over the moon about me starting to take an interest in myself again.

Scene Eleven

School corridor. Lunchtime. CLAIRE *approaches a classroom door which has a notice saying 'Meeting – girls only' on it. A lot of voices can be heard above the noise of a record which is playing in the background. The impression should be of about twelve girls in the room.*

CLAIRE (*opens the door*): Shut that thing off. (*The record player is turned off.*) What is the meaning of this? Now, get out of here and play tennis or something. Go on, file out of the other door quietly. Now. Not you, Diane, would you please come here?

Pause. DIANE *comes out of the room.* CLAIRE *shuts the door behind her, takes the notice off the door, folds it and hands it to* DIANE.

DIANE: Miss?

CLAIRE: Have you gone stark staring crackers?

DIANE: No.

CLAIRE (*now calm*): Let's talk sensibly about this.

DIANE: All right, you first.

CLAIRE (*firmly*): What is all this about?

DIANE: Haven't you read the school magazine?

MARION, *a pile of exercise books under her arm, crosses from left to right and comes within earshot of* DIANE's *next speech.*

CLAIRE (*noticing* MARION *and talking more softly*): Try to be . . .

DIANE (*angry*): No. I'm not going to try to be anything, least of all forcing myself to act normal. I hate the word, normal is a lie. You're always on about change, well I don't know about you, but I intend to change things.

Exit MARION.

CLAIRE: Standing in the dole queue won't change much. The only way to change the system is from within.

DIANE (*flatly*): Cop out.

CLAIRE: You think so?

DIANE: Every day making another compromise until you become so demoralised you hate yourself. (*Long pause.*) What about all those thousands of women who were burnt as witches? It was you who told us that it was because they were independent and men were frightened of them. (*Silence.* CLAIRE *still doesn't respond.*) What are you thinking?

CLAIRE: Something stupid, like how nice to be seventeen when the only dirty word is 'compromise'.

DIANE: You're only a generation away.

CLAIRE: A generation? Bloody cheek.

DIANE: You going to grass on us all then?

CLAIRE: I'm going to have to think about it.

DIANE: Thank you. (*Exit.*)

Enter MARION. *She crosses to* CLAIRE.

MARION (*conspiratorially*): I've notified Miss Grimble, she wants to see you in her office after school.

CLAIRE (*extremely angry, coldly*): Thank you, Marion. Do you not think I am capable of my own dirty work?

Scene Twelve

BEA's *office. Enter* CLAIRE.

BEA: Good work. I hear you caught the lot of them at lunchtime, in the act, I mean red-handed. I mean, you know, at this meeting, whatever. (*Pause. She starts again.*) Have you made a list of names?

CLAIRE: No.

BEA: Right, let's do that now. (*She pulls up a chair by the corner of the desk so they are sitting almost next to each other. She indicates* CLAIRE *to sit, which she does. Silence.*

CLAIRE (*slowly*): Miss Grimble.

BEA: Beatrice, my dear, in the confines of this room.

CLAIRE: Miss. Beatrice, Beatrice.

BEA: Yes?

CLAIRE: Do you think this is all really necessary?

BEA: Oh? Don't tell me all this will disappear by itself. That the Easter vac and a gorged dosage of chocolate egg wil put the equilibrium back in their defectiv hormones.

CLAIRE: It's just that we are committed to an anti-sexist policy in this school and . . .

BEA: We are, we are and I am the living proof of that, am I not? They wanted a man for this job. Oh yes, they did, you know. Ludicrous, isn't it? However, tha is an aside and nothing whatsoever to do with these rampant flauntings.

CLAIRE: But Miss Grim . . . Beatrice.

BEA: Call me Bea . . . all my friends do.

CLAIRE: I don't . . . it's a question . . . I feel we . . . that I, that is . . .

BEA (*kindly but with laboured patience*): Claire, it's Friday evening and I'm sure w both have better things to do. Now let's make a list of the names and get it over with. (*She picks up a pen.*) First off, Diane Collier, we all know that.

CLAIRE (*snaps*): No.

BEA: Come on now, she told me herself.

Long pause.

CLAIRE: You're going to have to put my name at the top of that.

Silence.

BEA (*stunned*): You mean? I hope you don't mean what I think you mean. Do you? I mean, what do you mean?

CLAIRE: Just that.

BEA (*shakes her head*): No.

CLAIRE (*nods her head*): Yes.

BEA: Hell fire, it's an endemic. (*Then:*) No no, you can't be, you're married and . . .

CLAIRE: Divorced. Don't you mean epidemic?

BEA: And you've got a little girl. What nonsense. I know what I mean, it's your vocabulary that's flagging.

CLAIRE: I left my husband to live with a woman. Anyway, it's not a disease of any descripton.

BEA: Yes, yes, plenty of women do that, doesn't mean a thing. Cheaper way to live. I'm all for frugal living.

CLAIRE: Because I wanted a relationship as well as . . .

BEA: Claire, let's just pretend you didn't say that.

CLAIRE: I don't feel any of us should have to pretend anything.

BEA (*sharply*): Are you still living with her?

CLAIRE: No, she . . .

BEA: And do you have a . . .

CLAIRE: No.

BEA (*relieved*): Well, then you're in the clear.

CLAIRE: Just because I don't have a lover doesn't mean I'm not a lesbian.

BEA (*quickly*): Still in my book you don't qualify to go on this piece of paper.

CLAIRE (*quietly*): Can't you see that I have to.

BEA: 'A man's got to do what a man's got to do.' Hardly seems the logical or appropriate cliché for your argument. Claire, I won't let you throw your career away like this.

Long pause.

CLAIRE (*tentatively*): You don't have to.

BEA: What option have you left me?

Pause.

CLAIRE: The same one I had.

BEA: I don't understand.

CLAIRE (*deep breath*): Forgive me. I think you do.

BEA: I'm all ears.

CLAIRE (*bravely*): Come on. Everyone knows you live with Miss Hemingford.

BEA: Really!! For your information Florrie's fiancé was killed in the war.

CLAIRE: That was forty-five years ago.

BEA: She was devoted to him. Absolutely devoted to him.

CLAIRE: I'm sorry but . . .

BEA: As well you might be. Marching in here suggesting that I am the Queen Bea of this business. I suppose according to you, we should get the authorities to rename this school 'The Mark of Cain'. There's a pun in there somewhere only I'm too angry to concoct it. Have you any idea of what you're saying?

CLAIRE: I think so.

BEA: Do you really expect me to take this on board?

CLAIRE (*clearly*): Yes. (*Slight pause.*) Yes, I do.

Long, long pause.

BEA (*quietly*): Florrie and I do live together but not for as long as you would think. Before that I had a very long-standing friend (*She corrects herself.*) relationship, but she died in a car crash in 1956.

CLAIRE: There really is no need.

BEA: Apparently there is. (*She shrugs.*) Long time ago now, probably the year you were born. I threw myself into my work and I am aware that I sail round this place with an air of bright bluffingly calm, occasionally desperate authority, but it is an act I can hide in and indeed at that time I relied on it for the sake of my sanity. I cannot afford to let myself get caught in the undertow. Do you understand?

CLAIRE: That. Yes. But, Bea . . .

BEA: After the accident she was in hospital for three weeks before she died. During that time my presence went unacknowledged. I wasn't allowed to see her. (*With irony.*) – only close family. And I was left with a sense of grief that couldn't be shared and an overwhelming feeling of utter – (*But she stops herself and then, firmly.*) And today, twenty-seven years later I am certainly not about to jeopardise my pension.

CLAIRE: But, I don't see . . .

BEA (*coldly*): So if you persist in this course of action you leave me very little alternative other than to ask for your resignation.

CLAIRE: You could sack me.

BEA: No, Claire, don't ask me to do that. Please think about it over the weekend.

CLAIRE: Will you?

Exit CLAIRE. BEA *is left grappling with her own guilt. A moment passes and she picks up the telephone and dials.*

BEA: Hello, it's only me. (*Pause, slightly irritated.*) Yes, of course I'm still here (*Pause.*) No, Florrie, I don't want to hear about the cat's paw now. (*Indignantly.*) Of course I'm all right, but I think perhaps I should get a cab to the governors' meeting tonight. (*Pause.*) It's got nothing to do with your driving. Oh, and in case anyone comes back for drinks be a dear and take that Natalie Barney print off the wall. (*Then.*:) I'll explain when I see you. Bye.

Immediate blackout.

Interval.

PART TWO

Scene One

CLAIRE *has collected* POPPY *from school. On their way home they have stopped to feed the ducks in the park.*

CLAIRE: Poppy, you're very quiet. Has something happened? (*Pause.*) Did you get told off today? (POPPY *shakes her head.*) Well, that's good. It wasn't swimming today, was it? We didn't forget your swimming things? (POPPY *shakes her head.*) You've not said much about the weekend. Tell me a bit more about the fair.

POPPY: It was okay.

CLAIRE: Poppy, what's the matter?

POPPY: I think I'm depressed.

CLAIRE: Oh dear. Why do . . .

POPPY (*blurts out angrily*): Dad said I was going to live at his house forever and that you were a filthy pike.

CLAIRE (*gently*): What did you say?

POPPY: I said, 'She hates fish and you can go stuff yourself.'

CLAIRE: Poppy!

POPPY: Well, you aren't dirty, I didn't tell him about you leaving your knickers in the sink.

CLAIRE: Did he say anything else?

POPPY: Yes, lots, I nearly forgot that I loved him.

CLAIRE: I know we've talked about this lot before, and you know I don't like your father much.

POPPY: He can't stand you either.

CLAIRE: That's sort of fair, isn't it?

POPPY (*agreeing*): S'pose so.

CLAIRE: And I left him when you were young and nobody ever asked you what you wanted.

POPPY: Huh, I was only a baby.

CLAIRE: Do you understand why all this happened?

POPPY (*flatly*): No, I don't.

CLAIRE (*smiles*): I mean what's happening?

POPPY: Dad is going to court because he wants me to live with him.

CLAIRE: Yes . . .

POPPY: But I've told everyone that I want to stay with you.

CLAIRE: And that's what I want – more than anything – but other people are going to decide for us.

POPPY: Why? It's none of their blimming business.

CLAIRE: Because your Dad won't give in and neither will I.

POPPY: I don't know why they're bothering because I'm staying put. Nobody can make me go.

CLAIRE: What I'm trying to say is that we don't have the power to decide.

POPPY: It's all such a mess.

CLAIRE: Yes. (*Smiles.*) You know, sometimes you sound just like your Nan.

POPPY: Why don't you and Nan have a fight with Dad? Nan would win 'cos she told me she keeps a Jif lemon in her handbag for muggers.

CLAIRE: Sometimes I don't know whose side she's on.

POPPY: Mine. I'd run away, you know. (*Emptying the last few crumbs from the bread bag. Then to the ducks:*) Okay, swim off. It's all gone.

CLAIRE: Perhaps we'll have a longer chat after supper. Do you want to go home?

POPPY: Yeah, the ducks are bored of us now.

Exit CLAIRE and POPPY, hand in hand.

Scene Two

Staff room. Lunchtime. MARION and ANNETTE are seated, packed lunches in Tupperware containers on their laps. CYRIL stares into space, a CND pamphlet in his hand. ROGER eats a banana. LINDA is mechanically bouncing a tennis ball against the wall.

ANNETTE: Frankly, I'm surprised she bothered to turn up at all.

MARION: The nerve. It was an oversight on Miss Grimble's part not to have suspended her in the first place.

ANNETTE: Linda, could you stop that please, the continuous thud, thud, thud is giving me a head.

LINDA *stops.*

MARION: She was obviously behind them.

LINDA *throws the ball once against the wall.*

ROGER (*with a mouthful of banana*): Surely that only applies to queer males.

ANNETTE: I'm sorry to have to say this, Roger, but your mouth should carry a government health warning.

Enter CLAIRE. Silence.

CYRIL: I must congratulate you on your new life, I never realised you had that sort of bent. Mind, it's very precarious trying to make a living out of the stage.

ROGER: No, Cyril, she's not a thesbian, you dozy cart-horse.

CYRIL: Oh, that's funny . . . there was this girl at college . . .

CLAIRE: Thanks, Cyril, but I don't bother with jock straps, not in the warm weather, you know.

CYRIL (*shrugs*): D'you know something, nobody ever bothered much about sex until 1960.

ANNETTE: People have been bothering about reproduction since long before you or I were born.

ROGER: We don't need any reminding. It's us that educates the product.

CYRIL (*incensed by the atmosphere*): Shall I tell you something, I might as well because I retire at the end of the summer term, and the nub of it is that I've hated every day of it.

ROGER: Steady on, Cyril.

CYRIL: Oh yes, and I know what they call me – Poly Mr Barrett, Polly Parrot and the only privilege I ever enjoyed was reading their names out of the detention book in assembly. I've seen generations of kids when all LSD meant to them was pounds, shillings and pence through the acid summer, when all that conjured up for them was litmus paper. Eras have come and gone. And what happens? They internalised the cliché of our times and spend their lives running scared. And whose fault is it then that they vote Tory? Ours.

ROGER: Not all of them are Conservatives.

CYRIL: Not for the want of ramming an ever-narrowing definition of choice down their necks so that it can be interpreted for 'status quo' and today, today, I took this (*Indicating the pamphlet.*) to discuss nuclear physics with the A level group and they looked at me as though I just announced the Pope had AIDs. All but two of them thought the nuclear deterrent absolutely necessary and those two are in Mrs Anderson's tutorial group. Teaching is supposed to be about enabling development to make choices, not being trained by a parrot to recite received information. I don't care what you are, Claire, you're a bloody good teacher, which is more than anyone will ever say of me – surgical support and all.

CYRIL *gets up – crosses to the door.*

ROGER: Where are you going?

CYRIL: Pub.

ROGER: I'll stand you a pint.

ROGER *and* CYRIL *exit.*

MARION: Seems the whole place is erupting. I for one can't loll about here all day. (*She gets up.*)

ANNETTE: Neither can I. (*Crossing to the door with* MARION.)

MARION *and* ANNETTE *exit, leaving the door ajar.*

LINDA: Was it worth it?

CLAIRE: I almost got a standing ovation from Cyril.

LINDA: So what? I didn't exactly see him making a bee line for Grimble's office.

CLAIRE: Or Roger Cunningham leaping up and down about NUT regulations.

LINDA: Actually, I don't know why they're here.

CLAIRE (*shrugs*): Nor do I. Except to give Annette and Marion something to cling on to.

LINDA: Them, they're so . . . words fail me . . .

CLAIRE: They do take the theory of false consciousness a bit far.

LINDA: That's a polite way of putting it.

CLAIRE: Marion is jealous – she thinks she should have been made acting deputy – and Annette is afraid.

LINDA: Yes, much too dangerous an atmosphere for the likes of us. Why did you do it?

CLAIRE: I was beginning to feel very guilty about being a Judas.

LINDA: I wouldn't have imagined you worrying about any character in the Bible.

CLAIRE: If I'd had the courage of those girls, at their age, everything would have been different.

LINDA: You think? This won't make any radical change except to the lives of those involved, they'll have to leave, eventually get one job, if they're lucky, after another, until they learn to conform. Go and explain to the Queen Bea that it was a mistake, an experiment, in pupil-teacher empathy.

CLAIRE: No. I've said what I've said.

LINDA: Now you're quoting Pontius Pilate, only at least he didn't crucify himself.

CLAIRE: All I did was tell the truth.

LINDA: Claire, please don't drag me into this. I couldn't cope.

CLAIRE: I'm not about to drag anyone anywhere.

LINDA: It would be much worse for me.

CLAIRE: How do you make that out?

LINDA: Use your head, I see them in the showers for Christsake, besides it would kill my mother.

CLAIRE: And I've got to fight for custody of my daughter.

LINDA: Christ, Claire, I didn't realise.

Enter ROGER. *He hovers. Exit* LINDA.

ROGER: Err, hi, you still here?

CLAIRE: No, this is an apparition. I thought you were supposed to be down the pub.

ROGER: I changed my mind. Claire, I know you won't believe me, but I'm sorry, I mean, I've always liked your spirit, always have, but I overheard about your daughter.

CLAIRE: You're the limit.

ROGER (*long pause*): Look, Linda, well, she's one thing, you're different.

CLAIRE: You're not . . .

ROGER: No, I've told you. Her secret's safe with me, you forget I'm one of the Rolling Stones generation. I've done things that would make your hair curl.

CLAIRE: Save it for your memoirs.

ROGER: Linda, well, it's obvious about her but you, I mean, you've been married, got a little girl, we all fancy a change from time to time. Monogamous sex can get boring.

CLAIRE: I'm sure you'll understand but I don't have any energy to put into your problems.

ROGER: Okay, I know you're bitter but I do like you. You must know I've always been attracted to you.

CLAIRE (*genuinely aghast*): I had no idea. I thought our feeling for each other was one of mutual dislike.

ROGER: Ah, this sad little boy's inability to express himself.

CLAIRE: Please spare me.

ROGER: Claire . . .

CLAIRE: Perhaps we could change the subject?

ROGER: Listen, if I was to say on oath in court that I was having a relationship with you, there would be no problem.

CLAIRE: You'd do that for me?

ROGER: Yes, I would. We'll have to go out to the pictures or somewhere and then the evidence would tally.

CLAIRE: I've misjudged you. (*She turns.*)

ROGER: And then perhaps depending on evidence, genuinely consummate it.

CLAIRE (*almost speechless with rage*): You bastard. (*She exits, slamming the door.*)

Scene Three

CLAIRE'*s living room.* POPPY, *in dressing-gown, sits on* CLAIRE'*s lap.*

POPPY: Can we get on with the story now?

CLAIRE: Where are we? (*Opening the book.*)

POPPY: We haven't even got to the bit about what they chose for themselves.

CLAIRE: Are you ready? (*She reads.*) Psyche went home to plead for a husband. Demeter and Persephone were astounded by such a strange desire, yet they knew it must be satisfied. In secrecy, for such a thing had never before happened, Psyche was married to Eros – to Love himself, to Cupid, Aphrodite's son. Psyche lived alone with her husband, in a splendid palace, set high on a nameless mountain. Silent, invisible servants brought her whatever she wished. At night, and only at night, Love came to visit: Psyche's husband, but she didn't know who he was or what he looked like. Love had warned her never to look at him, but to love him in ignorance.

POPPY (*sleepily*): What is ignorance?

CLAIRE: It means not knowing.

POPPY: Go on.

CLAIRE: Athena never returned to her mother's house. Instead she went straight to Zeus, the god of gods, and proposed a bargain much to his vain and clever liking: to be reborn of him. She asked him to become her mother. And so Athena became twice-born, the second time of a man. She emerged fully grown from Zeus's head, wearing the armour she so desired. This daughter of Demeter seemed to have no memory of her earthly female origins. (*Pause.*) Are you asleep?

POPPY (*almost asleep*): No, no. Go on.

CLAIRE: Artemis, the youngest of Demeter's daughters, returned to her mother's house. First she had Demeter consecrate her to the moon, so that no matter how far she'd have to wander, she would never forget, never betray. (*She looks at* POPPY.) Poppy? (POPPY *is asleep.*)

CLAIRE *carries* POPPY *out in her arms.* LAWRENCE *enters followed by* JEAN.

JEAN: She's upstairs with her daughter.

LAWRENCE: Good, excuse me.

JEAN *stands in front of the door.*

JEAN: She'll be down in a minute.

LAWRENCE: Let me past.

JEAN: Lawrence, you shouldn't be here at all.

LAWRENCE: Just keep out of this.

JEAN: Sit down if you must but you're not getting past me – not unless you want to appear twice in court on Friday.

LAWRENCE (*reluctantly sits down*): Your affidavit had better be good because we're going to make mincemeat out of the fact that you chose to live with a sordid pervert.

JEAN: (*moves away from the door*): I am quite capable of holding my own, Mr Anderson.

LAWRENCE: I'm sure you are.

JEAN: Look, Lawrence, Claire hasn't done anything wrong.

LAWRENCE: Oh no? Only turned my own daughter against me.

JEAN: That's not fair, she's always seemed very unbiased. Much more than I'd have been.

LAWRENCE: You just keep out of this or I'll drag you in in.

JEAN: Don't be ridiculous.

LAWRENCE: You won't be so smug if you get publicly labelled a 'practising lesbian ed.-psychologist'.

JEAN: I am practising as neither. I am a fully fledged educational psychologist and a sordid perverted heterosexual.

LAWRENCE: You'll have difficulty proving it.

JEAN: I have a well-oiled boyfriend.

LAWRENCE: That wimp from some 'Men Against Sexism' group. The only thing you two practise together is probably Yoga positions.

JEAN: In your position perjury is not going to . . .

Enter CLAIRE.

CLAIRE: Lawrence? What are you doing here?

LAWRENCE: A word with you. In private.

CLAIRE: It's all right, thanks, Jean.

Exit JEAN.

I think you've caused enough trouble.

LAWRENCE: Me? I've caused enough trouble?

CLAIRE: Yes, I didn't know you'd turned into a parrot.

LAWRENCE: It's not me who's taught Poppy to be foul-mouthed.

CLAIRE: I beg your pardon?

LAWRENCE: My own daughter, my own flesh and blood, told me, her own father, to get stuffed.

CLAIRE: She was upset.

LAWRENCE: So when she's upset she goes round telling everyone to get stuffed.

CLAIRE: I suppose you like her to bottle it all up, smile sweetly and pretend nothing's wrong, like your idea of the ideal model for adult behaviour.

LAWRENCE: She's too old for her years. The kid's had no life, no childhood. A mother who has no time for her.

CLAIRE: That's just not true, Lawrence, and you know it.

LAWRENCE (*calmly*): I'm only thinking of Poppy, believe me.

CLAIRE (*quietly but firmly*): Why don't you ask her what she wants?

LAWRENCE: Waste of time, you've well and truly poisoned her mind.

CLAIRE: That's not fair.

LAWRENCE: Too right it's not.

CLAIRE: I know we haven't turned out the best of friends.

LAWRENCE (*sourly*): Ha bloody ha.

CLAIRE: But I never thought it would turn out like this.

LAWRENCE (*wistfully*): It was you who thought happily ever after was a cheap empty dream.

CLAIRE (*quietly*): And I was right.

LAWRENCE: It didn't have to be like thät. I didn't go off with anyone else.

CLAIRE (*softly*): No.

LAWRENCE (*with total sincerity*): And I still miss you. You know, we had some good times together, didn't we? It wasn't all bad. You used to make me laugh. Sometimes, I still think you were the only real person I ever knew.

CLAIRE: Then why? Why put me through all this then?

LAWRENCE: Because I miss Poppy too. She's my daughter as well.

CLAIRE: But she's lived with me all this time, you agreed access when we got divorced.

LAWRENCE: I can give her so much more now and I want . . .

CLAIRE: You mean now you've got married again.

LAWRENCE: Yes, that's partly it.

CLAIRE: What can you give her, Lawrence, done purely out of motives of what you can take from me?

LAWRENCE: It will mean she'll have an ordinary home like other kids and not have to cope with snide remarks.

CLAIRE: She can fend for herself.

LAWRENCE (*reasonably*): Only because she doesn't know anything else. I love her.

CLAIRE (*firmly*): So do I.

LAWRENCE: I really don't want to put you through this, believe me.

CLAIRE: Then don't.

LAWRENCE: It's nothing to what you've put me through.

CLAIRE: Don't be so stupid.

LAWRENCE (*bitterly*): Always quick on the put-downs, weren't you? Well, we'll see just how well they stand up in front of an audience.

CLAIRE (*awkwardly*): Please, Lawrence, you know I'm not . . .

LAWRENCE (*with conviction*): You know I'm going to win.

CLAIRE: You know Poppy means everything to me. You can keep anything, take anything, but not this, let me keep Poppy.

LAWRENCE: It's up to the courts to decide now.

CLAIRE (*with quiet dignity*): You can change your mind. Anything else, you can have anything else.

LAWRENCE: Can I have you back?

CLAIRE: Oh, Lawrence. That's impossible.

LAWRENCE: Well, then. Can't you see I have to go through with it?

Exit.

CLAIRE: Lawrence?

The front door slams. Pause. Enter JEAN.

JEAN: You all right?

CLAIRE: Yes, I think so.

JEAN: What did he want?

CLAIRE: I don't really know.

JEAN: What happened?

CLAIRE: I don't really want to talk about it. How was your weekend?

JEAN: All right, what did you do?

CLAIRE: Oh, I saw Val.

JEAN: How is she?

CLAIRE: She'll be home by the weekend.

JEAN: That's good. What will she do?

CLAIRE: I'm not sure, I don't think she is either. I couldn't concentrate properly because it looks like I earned the sack.

JEAN: What?

CLAIRE: It's still a no-win situation. Miss Grimble refuses to sack me. I refuse to resign.

JEAN: What?! What for?

CLAIRE: A small matter of non-pacification over Diane Collier.

JEAN: Are you a complete babbling wally?

CLAIRE *looks at her.*

And for what – for one moment's satisfaction – riding high on the crest of a wave of martyred idealism.

CLAIRE (*coldly*): I can do without the objective heterosexist polemic. Thank you.

JEAN: Claire, in the name of whoever, you're supposed to stand before agents of the state.

CLAIRE: Agents of the devil.

JEAN: That they might be but they won't take too kindly to you telling them to go to hell – you've got to say what a responsible job you've got – how you've got everything going for you and you chuck it all up for a moment's unstable heroism.

CLAIRE: That might be how it appears to you. Anyway the court shouldn't find out unless Lawrence has hired tell-tale Marion Lansdowne as a private detective.

JEAN: For God's sake, Claire, compromise your principles.

CLAIRE: It' not a principle we're talking about. It's me. And what do you think I've done. I've compromised myself so much I've lied my way out of existence.

JEAN: Then why wreck it over some headstrong schoolgirl who probably wouldn't bother to turn round to thank you?

CLAIRE (*furious*): Wreck it? Wreck what? Something I've got very little hope of and absolutely no control over when the system dictates the outcome before the ushers clapped eyes on you. When welfare officers write down the names of books with the word 'woman' in the title and incriminate you. To be humiliated and ridiculed by a group of men and to gradually believe that the only thing that would change them is a bullet through the head. What sort of world is it where I have to plead for my own daughter?

JEAN: Claire.

CLAIRE (*angry*): And I will not calm down. I stand to lose Poppy and in the face of current opinion the only weapon I have is compromise and you think that's okay. And what the hell do you know, what difference does it make to you? None. None at all.

JEAN *does not respond.* CLAIRE *is too angry to apologise. Silence. The doorbell rings.* JEAN *exits.*

JEAN (*off*): Hello, Joyce.

JOYCE (*off*): Hello, Jean.

CLAIRE (*doesn't attempt to get up*): Oh no, please God no.

JEAN (*off*): Val's okay, I hear.

JOYCE (*off*): Yes, fine, she'll be home in a couple of days. Much more positive, so they tell me.

JEAN (*off*): That's good.

Enter JOYCE *with* JEAN. JEAN *exits, shutting the door behind her.*

JOYCE: Whenever I come round she goes out of the room.

CLAIRE (*snaps*): We share a house, not our relatives.

JOYCE: I saw Lawrence in his car as I was walking up the hill from the bus stop. I don't suppose he's reached a reconciliation?

CLAIRE: No, he bloody well hasn't and I don't want to hear a pack of rubbish about the sun shining out of his armpit either.

JOYCE: Well I never really got on that well with him, no not really. Certainly not after the divorce. He never even sends me a Christmas card now you know . . .

CLAIRE (*aggressively*): What do you want?

JOYCE (*very taken aback*): Claire . . .

CLAIRE: Oh stop dithering around and sit down now you're here.

JOYCE (*sits*): I haven't been able to sleep this week.

CLAIRE (*sarcastically*): Poor you.

JOYCE: I don't think I've had more than twelve hours sleep in the last fortnight. So I've been to see a solicitor.

CLAIRE: Can't you understand, I've got enough on my plate? I don't care about your neighbours, there's no law against

JOYCE (*firmly*): Look, Claire, I'm very sorry we had words. I can't stop thinking about it. I saw a solicitor about you.

CLAIRE: What for? To charge me with slander? (*A look from* JOYCE *is enough to make* CLAIRE *say:*) But Mum, I already have a solicitor.

JOYCE: I know that, don't I? This one specialised in custody, you should have got one who knew all about it in the first place.

CLAIRE (*through clenched teeth*): I have got one who deals with custody.

JOYCE: Yes, normal custody. Not one who deals with . . . you know . . . special circumstances.

CLAIRE (*firmly*): It's too late now Mum.

JOYCE (*sighs*): I just wish . . .

CLAIRE (*cutting her off*): It's no good bloody wishing, is it? Please get on with it.

JOYCE: The solicitor I saw was a specialist in . . .

CLAIRE: In special custody cases. Yes, you said that.

JOYCE: And on top of that, she was one of your lot as well.

CLAIRE (*deliberately provocative*): What, a teacher?

JOYCE: You know what I mean. (*Then quickly:*) Anyway she was very nice.

CLAIRE: She told you just like that.

JOYCE: No, I asked her outright, didn't I? Seemed a waste of time talking to one who wasn't and apart from that she had very good qualifications.

CLAIRE: She had to tell you that as well.

JOYCE: I could see that for myself, couldn't I? For one thing the sign on the door had so many letters on it there was hardly any room for the name.

CLAIRE (*flippantly*): Maybe we went to the same university.

JOYCE: Oh, I shouldn't wonder at all. I've always maintained that's where all those ideas come from. Those individual tutorials and seminal thingeys seem to lead to nothing but indulgent self-importance.

CLAIRE: So did you ask her?

JOYCE: Of course not. It's up to her own mother to find out where she went wrong.

CLAIRE: Which university she went to.

JOYCE (*becoming angry*): You what? You take the biscuit, you do, you're enough to try the patience of a saint. Do you know that? I haven't trailed half way across the country to find a whatname solicitor to ask which university she went to – just what sort of moron do you take me for?

CLAIRE: Can you get on with it because I can't understand a word you're saying.

JOYCE (*angry*): Just who do you think you are, girl? Eh? Just who? You've always been just a bit too quick with the backchat. You might find me ignorant, but if I hadn't made those sacrifices to get you the education that I never had, at least I wouldn't be made to feel small now by you and your clever talk. (CLAIRE *looks away but simultaneously mouths every word of the next sentence.*) That tongue of yours is so sharp that one day you'll cut yourself in half with it. (*Having caught a glimpse of* CLAIRE *out of the corner of her eye.*) Oh yes, and you think I'm shallow and boring and mentally rearranged.

CLAIRE (*winces*): I never said that.

JOYCE: Yes, but you've thought it. I've not had half of what you've had and it didn't fall out of the sky. I worked for it, only, only to have you march in so many years later on and announce with glee that you were living as man and wife with a woman and I'm trying to change, trying to explain to family and friends. For me and my lifetime, I've had to adapt much more than you ever have.

CLAIRE (*quietly*): It was hardly gleeful.

JOYCE: Whatever, whatever, it's much easier living in ignorance but it's not so awful, harder, painful even but not awful trying to understand. What is so awful is for all I've tried I get told to shut up and get lost.

CLAIRE (*softly*): I didn't.

JOYCE: You might as well have done. But when all's said and done, I'm still your mother and nothing is going to be able to change that for either of us.

CLAIRE (*smiles*): No.

JOYCE: And sleepless nights won't change anything, so I said to myself, Joyce, I said, worrying won't make it go away, get off your behind and do something, so I went to the top set of chambers they call them to find a solicitor.

CLAIRE: So far so good. I'm with you.

JOYCE: And I said if it was your daughter and your granddaughter, what would you advise them to do?

Pause.

CLAIRE (*gently*): Yes.

JOYCE: She told me to tell you both to skip the country.

CLAIRE (*flatly*): I hope you didn't pay for that advice.

JOYCE: As it happens I didn't have to, no. But I was more than willing to, I might add, and for your information that's just what you're going to do.

CLAIRE: Don't be so . . . so . . . we'll just hitch out to the airport, and say what with having to appear in court and all would they just fly us out of the way. And where did you think we should go to?

JOYCE: Just hold your horses and while you're about it, that tongue of yours as well.

CLAIRE (*ignoring this*): Where? And where have you thought we'd go?

JOYCE: America.

CLAIRE: America??!!

JOYCE: I know it can't be done just like that. God knows you don't get nothing in this life that easily. (*Deep breath.*) So I had a long chat with Sybil and she will arrange everything that end and I've spoken to Mrs Cuthberts downstairs, you know, the one with the son who manages the travel agents and he can get the plane ticket and visa and I went to the bank to see about travellers cheques.

CLAIRE (*exasperated*): But Mum.

JOYCE: And I've been to the building society today and I want you to have it. (*She takes out an envelope and puts it in CLAIRE's lap.*) That's all I wanted to say.

JOYCE *gets up to go.* CLAIRE *gently takes hold of* JOYCE's *wrist so her mother remains where she is. Long pause.*

CLAIRE (*almost inaudibly*): But Mum.

JOYCE (*stickily*): We have our differences – we'll probably have them until the day die, but I do know this much, if we didn't have them, Lawrence wouldn't be able to use them to get back at you.

CLAIRE (*hands back the envelope. JOYCE will not take it. CLAIRE puts it on the floor between them*): I can't. (*Slight pause.*) You'd do this for me? (*Pause.*) There are laws, that would give them the power to bring us back.

JOYCE: They'll have to find you first, and all the time they're looking will cost Lawrence money and mark my words, he'll give up. If not, in a couple of years Poppy's age will make sure he has no say in the matter.

CLAIRE: And just what do I tell Poppy? That's no way to bring her up, living as a fugitive.

JOYCE: Fugitive nothing and it won't be the rest of your life, will it? It's only to see you over. You always over-dramatise things. How are you going to explain to Poppy anyway, Lawrence has everything to back him up. You've got to play a game by somebody else's rules just to keep her with you, which you both want but are unlikely to get.

CLAIRE (*flatly*): I think I've got to go through with it.

JOYCE: Why? Seems to me that nobody cares what a good mother you are. All they care about is the other thing. And wearing a dress from Marks and Spencer on the day is hardly likely to fool anyone either. And what about that welfare officer? No sooner was my foot in the door when this voice booms 'And what do you feel about your daughter's homosexuality?' And I said, 'Could be worse, she could be dead.' Well, it was a joke, wasn't it, only every word got written down.

CLAIRE: Look, once in court I can take that report apart and show it up for what it is.

JOYCE (*agreeing*): I'm sure, I'm sure, and who will they believe? A lot rests on these people. No, look, it's taken me long enough to come round and I'm your mother so you're hardly going to persuade some Hurray Henry judge with a broom handle up his backside, to your way of thinking, not in an afternoon anyway.

CLAIRE: No, I won't give in. If there's one thing I've learnt from you it's stand my ground and fight.

JOYCE: And if there's one thing I didn't teach it was to sink. This time you're up to your neck in quicksand and wrenching your own head won't help. You need a hand – somebody else's. Before you say anything, Sybil said that.

CLAIRE: Typical Sybil line that is. It's not what I want.

JOYCE: I don't want it either but it seemed to me that only by letting go of the two of you could any sort of solution be found.

CLAIRE: Thank you, Mum, but I can't.

Scene Four

BEA's *living-room.* BEA *shows* DIANE *and* TERRI *in.*

BEA: This really isn't on, you know. If you wanted to see me you should have come to my office.

TERRI: We wanted to talk to you urgently.

BEA: How did you know where I lived?

DIANE: The phone book.

BEA: I see. Well, now you're here, sit down.

DIANE *and* TERRI *sit nervously on the edge of the settee.*

But I'm not in the mood to listen to threats and ultimatums so if that's what you're about you can walk right out again.

TERRI: No, we realised that we'd done a lot of damage.

BEA: I'm listening. I would offer you a cup of tea only the water is temporarily cut off.

DIANE: We overheard something about Mrs Anderson.

FLORRIE (*shouts off*): Bea? Would you be a darling and bring me an adjustable spanner?

BEA (*gets up quickly, shouts*): One minute. (*To* DIANE *and* TERRI:) My lodger is changing a washer.

FLORRIE (*shouts off*): Thanks, darling.

BEA: Excuse me. (*Once out of the door we hear* BEA *charging up the stairs.*)

DIANE: Fancy calling your landlady darling.

TERRI: Must work in the theatre. They all do that.

CLAIRE: Yeah. (*She ges up and starts looking around the room.*)

TERRI: Sit down. If she finds you poking your nose into anything she'll throw us out.

DIANE: We'll know when she's coming back. She couldn't have made more noise going up the stairs if she'd tried.

TERRI (*gets up and surveys the bookcase*): Boring, boring, boring.

DIANE (*finds a small framed photograph behind a plant*): Hey, look at this, an old photo of Bea with her arm round a woman.

TERRI (*looking at the photo*): They all did that then. Gawd, look at those shoes.

DIANE: She's still got them by the sound of it. (*She opens the desk drawer and tentatively rummages around its contents.*)

TERRI (*alarmed*): Don't do that.

DIANE: She poked her nose into our lives.

TERRI: We shoved our lives under her nose, you mean.

DIANE (*pulls out a card*): Look, an anniversary card.

TERRI: Blimey. Maybe she was married then.

Both of them look at it.

DIANE (*reads*): What can I say after twelve years except –

TERRI: Don't read it out loud, it's embarrassing.

They both read it.

TERRI ⎱ (*exclaim in unison*): All my
DIANE ⎰ love, Florrie.

They look at each other.

TERRI ⎱
DIANE ⎰ Miss Grimble's one.

*Their discovery causes such elation that
they jump and dance around the room,
hugging each other, proclaiming 'Miss
Grimble's one' until the sound of* BEA
*clumping, in a rather more dignified
manner, down the stairs.* DIANE *throws
the card back in the drawer and shuts it.
They sit on the settee as before. Enter*
BEA.

BEA: I'm sorry about that. Now where
were we? (DIANE *and* TERRI *just sit
and stare at her slightly open-mouthed.*)
Mrs Anderson. Now what d'you know of
Mrs Anderson's business?

DIANE: Mrs Anderson. Yes. Ummmm.
We didn't realise about her custody case.

BEA: And how did you find out about it?

TERRI: We accidentally – (*She stops
herself.*) – we were eavesdropping, Miss
Grimble.

DIANE (*having recovered herself*): In fact,
we're thinking of setting up a a detective
agency.

TERRI (*to* MISS GRIMBLE): We had to
tell you about it. (*To* DIANE:) Be quiet,
Diane.

BEA: Actually, Linda, Miss Fellows, put
me in the picture this afternoon.

DIANE: We've come to make a bargain.

TERRI: She means to be flexible and
apologise.

BEA: But what can I do?

DIANE: Go to court and testify for Mrs
Anderson.

BEA: I don't know about that.

FLORRIE (*shouts off*): Water's back. Shall
I put the kettle on?

DIANE: Two sugars for me, please,
Florrie. Ta.

TERRI (*nudges* DIANE): Shush.

DIANE *grins.*

Scene Five

Outside the courtroom. Before CLAIRE *is
about to enter the room. Enter* BEA .

BEA: Claire? Claire?

CLAIRE: Miss Grimble. What are you
doing here?

BEA: I had no idea. Why didn't you tell
me?

CLAIRE: How did you find out?

BEA: It's too long a story to unravel just
now.

CLAIRE: I hope you've not come here to
be defamatory about my character.

BEA: Quite the opposite. In fact, if I'd
known about this I'd have made a change
in direction earlier in the day.

CLAIRE: Meaning what?

BEA: I'm here to offer what support I can.

CLAIRE: Thank you. (*Pause.*) And what
of Diane *et al*?

BEA: I'm still negotiating with them. Oh,
absolutely no question of expulsion. We
are simply haggling over the new section
of the history syllabus. But I'm very much
hoping for a settlement on the word
'spinsters'. But first things first. I've
explained to your barrister that should it
be necessary I will testify to the fact that
you are my deputy and an excellent
teacher.

CLAIRE: Thank you.

BEA: Whatever else. I do understand about
loss especially when it can go
unrecognised or without a glimmer of
sympathy from those around you.

CLAIRE: I've got a lot on my side, a good
home and career and, if I say so myself,
I'm a very good mother.

BEA: You're not going to be judged on the
quality of your parenting but on the basis
of your sexuality.

Fade. Lights up on LAWRENCE *and his
barrister. A* FEMALE CLERK *hovers in
the background.*

BARRISTER: When we win, will you take
your little girl straightaway?

LAWRENCE: No, tomorrow morning will
suit me better. Do you actually think it's a

foregone conclusion?

BARRISTER: Everything's in your favour. (*To the* CLERK:) Be a love and get an extra copy of the welfare officer's report.

Exit CLERK.

LAWRENCE: Even so, she is her mother, I suppose.

BARRISTER (*drily*): Now is not the time to doubt her parentage. (*Then:*) Mr Anderson, you must be prepared to explain everything to the court, if necessary in the detail in which you first relayed it to me, and then we will have dismantled every right she thought was hers.

LAWRENCE: I was extremely angry when I first sought your advice.

BARRISTER: But you still want your daughter.

LAWRENCE: Yes.

BARRISTER: Therefore you will have to be prepared to 'throw the book' at your ex-wife. (*Pause.*) Well?

LAWRENCE (*firmly*): Yes.

BARRISTER: Good. Then our case is watertight.

CLERK OF THE COURT (*voice off*): Custody Case Number Thirty-Seven – Anderson versus Anderson.

Fade. Lights on VAL.

VAL: I think now, that I knew I was getting ill, losing control. I remember when the boys were just babies and we lived in hard-to-let flats with the railway track running behind our block and lifting one of them up to see a train go past – it all seems so insignificant now. He was fascinated and as I held him I started to cry and repeat over and over 'This is a little person'. I felt happy and overwhelmingly sad at the same time, I don't know why and from then on it was like getting drunk. No, nothing dramatic, like swinging naked from chandeliers, not that I suppose I wouldn't have been tempted had any swung my way – like when you start to get drunk, you relax, tell yourself you can sober up in a minute, only you can't and when confronted with sober people you know you're losing ground, so you appear more drunk, not

that you could appear sober if you wanted to anyway. It's very difficult to remember being unhappy – the actual feeling, like when you're freezing cold in the middle of winter – you can remember lying on the beach boiling hot but you can't imagine enough to feel it. And when you're lying in the sun you can only remember being cold but not what it felt like. (*Pause.*) I haven't got an old self. I haven't got a new self to be cast on and off like a winter and summer coat. What I am is me.

JUDGE (*voice off*): Custody, care and control awarded to the natural father, Lawrence Anderson.

Lights up on CLAIRE *and* JOYCE.

JOYCE: Nobody would believe that anyone above those appointed to sit in judgement could ask such filthy questions. Those people are obsessed, they must be sick in the head. I might have difficulty saying the word lesbian but nobody makes me ashamed for loving my own daughter.

LAWRENCE *crosses in front of them.*

LAWRENCE (*to* CLAIRE): First thing tomorrow morning and have everything ready.

Scene Six

VAL, *ready to go home. Enter* NURSE.

NURSE: I'm just about to go off duty but your sister rang up with this message. (*She hands her a piece of paper.*) From New York. I hope it's not bad news.

VAL (*reads the note than looks up*): No, not in the circumstances.

NURSE: Val, I just wanted to say . . .

Enter the OLDER DOCTOR.

DOCTOR: Looking forward to going home, Mrs Jones?

VAL: I'm looking forward to leaving here.

DOCTOR: Now, you know where we are, should you ever need us. Must take it easy when you get home, not rush things, but I'm sure Dr March has explained that to you.

VAL: Yes, Doctor.

DOCTOR: Good. (*He looks at his watch.*) What time did your husband say he'd collect you?

VAL: My mother's taking me home.

DOCTOR: Right, I see. Well, I'd better go before I'm tempted to make a quip about women not being renowned for punctuality.

The sound of furious knocking on a door can be heard.

LAWRENCE (*off*): Come on. Open the bloody door. It's no use stalling for time.

DOCTOR: What on earth is that noise?

Neither VAL or the NURSE have heard anything and both look blankly at him.

NURSE: What noise?

DOCTOR: Sounds like someone is pulling the whole place apart. Come with me. (*He turns to exit.*) All the very best then, Mrs Jones. (*Exit. The NURSE reluctantly follows.*)

VAL (*looking at the note again*): Poppy and Claire have arrived safely and Sybil sends her love.

Lights up on LAWRENCE trying to kick CLAIRE's front door down.

LAWRENCE (*shouts*): For the last time, open this door, Claire.

Then fade. Lights up on VAL. Enter JOYCE.

JOYCE (*holds out her hand to VAL*): Ready?

VAL (*taking her mother's hand*): Yes.